ESSENTIAL LAW
FOR SOCIAL WORKERS

ESSENTIAL LAW
FOR SOCIAL WORKERS

ROBERT G. MADDEN, L.C.S.W., J.D.

COLUMBIA UNIVERSITY PRESS ■ NEW YORK

Columbia University Press
Publishers Since 1893
New York   Chichester, West Sussex

© 2003 Columbia University Press
All rights reserved

Library of Congress Cataloging-in-Publication Data
Madden, Robert G.
Essential law for social workers / Robert G. Madden.
p.   cm.
Includes bibiliographical references and index.
ISBN 0–231–12320–5 (cloth : alk. paper)—ISBN 0–231–12321–3 (paper : alk. paper)
1. Social workers—Legal status, laws, etc.—United States.   I. Title.

KF390.S6M33 2003
340'.024'362—dc21
2003043515

Columbia University Press books are printed
on permanent and durable acid-free paper.
Printed in the United States of America
c 10 9 8 7 6 5 4 3 2 1
p 10 9 8 7 6 5 4 3 2 1

To my father, who died during the time that I was writing this book:

You taught me that family and friends are my most important resource.
You provided me with a model of how to be a good father, husband, and person.
You inspired me to enjoy life and to balance all its demands.

CONTENTS

Acknowledgments ix
Introduction xi

1. Why Social Workers Study the Law: Knowledge for Practice 1

Participation in the Legal System 1
The Nature of the Law 2
Learning About the Law 11
Inductive Reasoning: From Practice Problems to Legal Principles 15

2. Exploring Jurisprudence: Legal Philosophy 17

Naturalism 18
Legal Positivism 21
Schools of Legal Thought 22
Recent Legal Reform Movements 33

3. The Development of the Law 39

Judicial, Legislative, and Administrative Processes 39
Comparing Criminal and Civil Law Procedures 48
The Structure of the Court System 50
Rules and Cases: Common Law Development 54

4. The Practice of Law 58

The Advocacy System and the Roles of Legal Professionals 58
Introduction to Legal Reasoning 68
Legal Knowledge for Social Workers 71

5. The Litigation Process: Dissecting a Court Case 77

The Stages of a Lawsuit or Criminal Trial 78

6. Protection of Individuals and the Preservation of Social Order 96

Constitutional Protections and American Values 96
Criminal Law and Criminal Procedure 104
Influencing Legal Policy 107

7. How Courts Make Legal Decisions About People's Lives 108

Balancing Legal Rights and Social Needs 108
The Process and Orientation of Family and Juvenile Courts 110
The Process and Orientation of Probate Court 118
Judicial Responses to Social Problems 121

8. Torts: How the Law Provides Compensation for Injury and Deters Unsafe Practices 124

Elements of Negligence and Malpractice Actions 125
Intentional Torts 129
Benefits to Social Work Practice 130

9. Contracts and Other Legal Issues in the Management of Social Work Practice 131

Basic Principles of Contract Law 131
Contracts with Clients: Informed Consent 135
Contracts with Managed-Care Organizations 135
Legal Issues in Agency Management 137
Legal Issues in the Business of a Private Practice 142

Appendix: Legal Research 151

Statutory Law 151
Case Law 152
Electronic Legal Research 154

References 157
Cases and Laws Cited 167
Index 169

ACKNOWLEDGMENTS

To my family, Doreen, Bryant, and Kyle, for your support and love.

To my friends Charlotte Pinto and Raymie Wayne, whose careful reading of earlier and lesser versions of this manuscript has greatly improved the clarity and content of the final product—thanks.

To my students and colleagues at Saint Joseph College and all who have attended my courses, trainings, and workshops: your case examples, questions, encouragement, and thoughts on how law and social work intersect gave me the insight and courage to write a book about the law without losing my social work identity.

Finally, to Polly Kummel, copy editor extraordinaire, whose clear thinking and assertive editing enriched the language and flow of this book.

INTRODUCTION

As I HAVE traveled around, giving workshops and teaching courses about legal issues in social work practice, I have come to realize that social workers need to learn more about the law itself rather than merely learning how to follow legal mandates. How do lawyers think? What is legal reasoning? What legal philosophy guides the decisions of a court? What is the purpose of arcane legal rules and procedures? What are the legal ramifications of following one course of action over another?

Previously, I have written and lectured about the ways that social workers can respond to the legal issues attendant to practice. In this book I have tried to deconstruct the law itself, to uncover the foundation of legal thinking and reasoning in order to demystify the law. My hope is that social workers will be able to use this legal knowledge to work more effectively in legal settings and to feel more confident about encounters with lawyers. Social workers are charged with the duty to be advocates for clients in legal systems and to consider ways to work for changes in legal processes to make them more therapeutic for all members of society. These goals can best be met by social workers who have a thorough understanding of the legal system and the legal concepts that support it.

This book begins with a broad perspective on the philosophical and historical foundations of the U.S. legal system. Social workers must be aware of these elements to appreciate the significance of structures, rules, and roles in the practice of law. I have included chapters that describe legal reasoning and the stages of litigation in order to provide social workers with knowledge of how to manage their involvement with legal systems. The material on constitutional law presents an overview of individual rights, essential information for social workers committed to social justice. Finally, the last three chapters explore practical legal issues commonly encountered in social work practice, such as family law, probate matters, malpractice, and business law for private practice.

Preston-Shoot (1997) identifies four distinct but interrelated strands of social work and the law: First, statutes and regulations grant legal powers and duties to social workers. These laws provide guidance concerning the scope of social workers' power and discretion to make practice decisions. Second, the profession has developed ethical guidelines and professional practice rules specifying the standards of care that social workers should abide by in their practice. Third, consumer complaints to courts and administrative agencies alleging misconduct or negligence enable a review of the actions of social workers and social services agencies, further defining specific duties and expectations for professional behavior. Finally, social welfare laws establish the rules, resources, and eligibility guidelines for social programs that provide services to people. These laws detail the role and scope of discretion for social workers who are providing social services under these rules. These four strands affect the practice of social work, and all social workers should become literate in the law in each area. Categorizing the sources of social work law in this manner enables social workers to conceptualize the purpose and scope of the law and thereby to become empowered through increased knowledge and understanding.

Part of the difficulty with learning about the law is the complexity of these legal sources and difficulty with the language, style, and accessibility of legal information. Many social workers have an expectation that the law can provide specific guidance concerning what course of action to take in a practice decision. Should I breach confidentiality when a client is not acting safely? Should I terminate a client who has not paid his bill for months? Should I disclose when a client is hiding assets in order to be eligible for an assistance program? The discomfiting truth is that the law will not answer most practice dilemmas of this sort with a conclusive opinion. Instead, social workers need to understand the law as a set of principles that can help them to meet the expectations of reasonable professional behavior. When social workers analyze a practice issue from this knowledge base, the result is a more empowered and confident course of action.

In many circumstances the law gives social workers power to act under legal authority. Understanding these legal powers and responsibilities allows social workers to use discretion to effectively meet the needs of their clients. This knowledge allows social workers to inform clients of options and to offer services in a safe, fair, and just manner, thereby increasing client cooperation and empowerment. This knowledge also allows social workers to use professional judgment confidently within the authority provided under the law.

Knowledge of the law helps social workers to judge the scope of their discretion. Social work discretion includes both the substantive requirements of a particular program or service and the selection of methods, the development of the treatment plan, and many other practice decisions. Knowledge of the law also helps social workers to develop specific language for describing their practice to legal systems, to champion clients' rights, and to retain control of essential decisions in practice.

It is important to understand a basic truth about the law. By its nature the law is a defender of the status quo, the power structure in U.S. society. Yet the law is an important context for social change. The law reflects American values of justice and equality while simultaneously reflecting social, racial, and economic myths and prejudices. This apparent dichotomy is an essential truth that social workers must understand in order to be players in the legal system. Social justice and civil rights are the tools within the legal system for balancing certain democratic processes (for example, those that reflect the views of the majority) that are less likely to allow changes that benefit dispossessed groups. The lack of money, power, influence, and organization create an impossible barrier to consistent and fair hearings by legislators and policy makers. Change on behalf of disfavored groups and individuals is possible only when they have advocates, information, and access to the legal system.

What is the proper legal role for social workers? The National Association of Social Workers' *Code of Ethics* requires social workers to challenge social injustice (1999). The law provides an environment within which social workers can fulfill this mandate. The legal system also provides the context within which social workers can serve as advocates for clients and causes. Currently, social workers underuse the legal system as a tool for advocacy and social change. I hope that the legal insights gained from this book, combined with a commitment to a broader study of the law, will guide social workers to become confident and competent legal advocates.

ESSENTIAL LAW
FOR SOCIAL WORKERS

1.

WHY SOCIAL WORKERS STUDY THE LAW: KNOWLEDGE FOR PRACTICE

A new world is only a new mind. —William Carlos Williams

THERE IS LAW in all social work practice. As tempting as it may be to deny or ignore this essential truth, social work practice in contemporary society requires knowledge of the law and legal systems. Consciously or not, every social worker participates in legally influenced practice in all practice settings and must be prepared to work with legal professionals to support clients, to try to change the system, and to foster appropriate practice standards. Social workers who open their minds to legal reasoning will find a range of opportunities to improve their practice.

PARTICIPATION IN THE LEGAL SYSTEM

States and professional organizations regulate social work practice by issuing credentials and sanctioning those who fail to meet legally defined standards of care. Clients may be involved with various legal systems such as juvenile, criminal, family, or probate courts. State and federal statutes place social workers in the role of interpreting and applying the law in such areas as immigration, adoption, civil rights, and welfare services. Social workers may be asked to provide information to legal officials in the form of professional records, testimony, or expert opinion. Some social work professionals work directly in legal settings, and their forensic practice requires a thorough understanding of the law.

The nature of law is a subject that has filled many bookshelves, but few volumes are accessible to social workers. Many social work authors have written about the legal dimensions of social work issues, such as confidentiality (Dickson 1998), psychotherapy practice (Madden 1998), child welfare (T. Stein 1991), and malpractice (Houston-Vega, Nuehring, and Daguio 1997), but few have explored the essential nature of the law, legal reasoning, or the practice of law.

Perhaps the focus of the social work profession—on interpersonal skills and being nonjudgmental—makes study of the law intimidating, or at least uncomfortable, for the average social worker. Instead, social workers seem to fall back on two disempowering myths when dealing with legal issues: the first views the legal world as a closed system in which the only people who can function there are those who have been through the rigors of a proper law school education. The second myth is that the law consists of clear legal mandates that define how people should act. Jansson, describing similar dynamics that occur within a broader policy context, refers to the former as the "expert myth" and to the latter as the "myth of powerlessness" (1994:21). These myths influence social workers' interactions with the law and legal systems, making us passive and reactive.

It would be inconceivable for a social worker practicing with children not to understand child development. Equally unsettling would be a social worker in a long-term care facility who was not thoroughly grounded in geriatric medical conditions. Just as child development theory and medical knowledge inform the judgments of social workers, so must legal theories inform the daily practice decisions of social workers. Yet the social work profession has tacitly enabled practitioners to enter practice without sufficient knowledge of the law and the skills for effective participation in legal systems (Madden 2000b).

When social workers have knowledge of legal processes and legal structures, they find the nature of legal interactions less intimidating, and they are more likely to become active participants in the development and application of the law as it relates to the lives of clients and the practice of social work. In a classic article Charlotte Towle argued for the union of cause and function in social work (1961). It is not enough to be caring and committed to social change (cause), without combining it with intellectual concepts, methods, and standards of practice (function). The law can be an instrument to promote the cause and function of social work. For social workers to be effective advocates and proponents of social justice, they must have technical legal knowledge and skills.

THE NATURE OF THE LAW

The law isn't justice. It's a very imperfect mechanism. If you press exactly the right buttons and are also lucky, justice may show up in the answer. A mechanism is all the law was ever intended to be.　　　　—Raymond Chandler

As social work has evolved as a profession and society has become more litigious, practitioners increasingly are aware of the need for more knowledge of the law (Barker and Branson 2000). But what is the law and what knowledge do social workers need? Sunstein suggests that the critical role for a well-functioning legal system is to develop a strategy for producing stability and agreement in the midst of social disagreement and pluralism (1996:4).

It would be comforting to think about the law as a system that defines the rights and obligations of each citizen in a way that reflects integrity, equality, and justice. When we view the law from this noble but inadequate premise, we can think about it as something that exists separately from daily life, to be applied by legal professionals. Instead, I will argue that the law frames social work practice with legal rules and mandates. If we accept the more mundane view, that the law is principally a mechanism to enforce the values of and structure relationships in an ever-changing society, social workers must learn to be consumers of legal principles, able to apply the law to our practice experiences. Further, we must learn to be legal architects and engineers, influencing the design and implementation of legal rules and procedures to benefit clients and the profession.

It is important to note that I am not seeking to make social workers into lawyers but to make social workers appreciate basic legal analysis, to understand concepts of jurisprudence, and to gain competence in the workings of the legal system. If social workers learn to think like a lawyer, their experiences with the legal system will be less stressful and more productive. The legal framework of practice will have real meaning and can inform practice decisions in the same way that other normative theories contribute to social work knowledge.

What does the phrase "to think like a lawyer" mean? Once we cast aside the urge to respond to this question with a punch line, it presents a formidable challenge. Vandevelde (1998) describes the process of legal thinking as both a goal-directed activity and a method. The initial goal of legal thinking is to identify the rights and duties of the people or entities involved in a factual situation. The lawyer's method includes identifying and analyzing relevant law and applying the legal rules and their underlying policies to the facts of a case (Vandevelde 1998:1–3).

When lawyers are presented with a factual situation, legal thinking guides their response. When social workers confront legal situations, social work values frequently determine their response. The difference can lead to miscommunication and distrust between social workers and legal professionals. Consider the case of a psychotherapy group facilitated by a licensed social worker that operated as part of the inpatient services at a mental health facility. A client, John, was part of this group during his hospitalization in 1996. During a group meeting another member of the group assaulted John, who suffered injuries. Sometime later John tried to sue his assailant but did not know the group member's name. John's lawyer tried to compel the mental health facility to disclose the identity of the assailant. The legal question in this case was whether the social worker–client privilege prevented the disclosure of the group member's identity (*Falco v. Institute of Living* [2000]).

From a lawyer's perspective the case involves a legal rule: the privileged communication statute. The lawyer for each party would carefully review the language of the state law and analyze the language of the statute and the facts to assess the strength of the client's legal case:

1. Does the statute apply to this social worker and this agency?
2. Is there a duty of confidentiality owed to a client in a psychotherapy group? If there is, are all communications within the group protected by the privilege?
3. Would a release of information limited to the client's name and address violate the statute?
4. Do any of the exceptions to the statute that allow for release of information without the client's consent apply to the facts of this case?

The lawyers would seek to determine the policy goals of the privileged communication legislation and attempt to frame their legal argument within these goals. How the statute is written determines how the law balances the legal principle of unfettered access to relevant evidence with the competing legal principle of protecting the privacy of people in mental health treatment. Based on this analysis, and an examination of how similar cases have been decided, each lawyer would attempt to predict how the court would rule.

A competent attorney representing the injured person could construct a plausible argument supporting disclosure, while a competing attorney representing the agency could develop an equally persuasive argument against disclosure. John's lawyer may argue that the language of the statute, the intent of the legislature, public policy, or general notions of fairness direct the court to order the release of the information. The focus of the argument would rest on the premise that the information being sought does not concern sensitive, personal content but only the identity of an individual who may have caused harm. The privileged communication statute should not be used to shield this wrongdoer from responsibility for his actions.

The lawyer for the agency may argue that the privilege statute applies to the case. This argument prioritizes the privacy rights of all mental health clients.

Because the statute specifically lists when a court is allowed to override the privilege statute, the lawyer could argue that the facts do not fall within any of the exceptions, so the judge must deny the request to provide the identity of the group member. To decide otherwise could have a negative effect on the promise of confidentiality that is fundamental to the willingness of clients to engage in treatment.

The social worker may experience the case as an intrusion into the therapeutic promise of confidentiality and its importance for the development of trust. The social worker views the act of identifying a client as a serious breach of privacy because of the frequent discrimination practiced against people who receive mental health services. Like the agency's attorney, the worker may worry about the effect of this case on people's participation in therapy groups. The social worker may question the validity of the lawsuit, especially if the physical attack was not seen as severe enough to cause lasting injuries. The social worker may also have self-serving reasons to conceal the identity of the group member: if this case never goes to court, the social worker will not have to give depositions or testify.

SOCIAL WORKERS' EXPERIENCES WITH THE LAW

The social worker simply may want a clear answer: "Just tell me what the law says about this type of situation." As I will discuss in later chapters, the law usually does not work as we would like it to. It does not provide us with simple answers to legal disputes except in the most obvious matters. Even in the case of taking the life of another person, the law allows for different penalties if the act that led to the death was intentional, negligent, or justifiable, as in self-defense. Courts have the role of applying the written law. Despite policies aimed at encouraging courts to decide similar cases in the same way, variation from case to case is surprisingly frequent.

As social workers, we are uncomfortable with the uncertainty of what appear to be incomplete laws and conflicting cases. Wouldn't it be more predictable and just if legal rules were more complex, stating the desired outcome in every situation? The reality is that a more complex legal code would provide illusory benefits (Epstein 1995). Too many factual situations push at the boundaries and language of a rule, making the task of compiling a comprehensive legal code impossible.

As the world changes, the need for new laws to deal with unanticipated factors is constant. Should we expect the legislature to adjust the language of its statutes each time technology advances? No matter how carefully a law is written, the interests of justice might require a result that appears on its face to contradict the law directly. For these reasons, no specific legal rule governs many practice situations, and sometimes even where a legal rule seems to exist, an alternative result is possible.

Any attempt to examine the law in its pure forms results in unsatisfying encounters. Because of this, examining the law as inseparable from its functions is pedagogically more useful (Albert 2000). How does the law operate to protect individuals, to settle conflicts between parties, or to determine the rights or obligations of people? How does the law reflect social values and enforce moral standards? Social workers can understand the law most effectively when it is applied to familiar situations. Therefore this book uses cases and situations from social work practice for analyzing the law and extracting legal principles. Whether the court in a particular case has ignored these legal principles or found them to be crucial, they will provide social workers with insight and direction when they face legal issues in practice.

Although legal scholarship and judicial decision making rely on multiple sources of legal reasoning, this book will focus on how to learn legal principles by understanding the reasoning of particular cases. Throughout the book I present cases that illustrate the general legal rules and principles of importance to social work practice.

The case vignettes that follow are examples of social workers in dynamic interactions with legal issues. In each case the facts support the need for social workers in diverse practice settings to develop an understanding of the law and the legal system. The social worker who has a foundation of legal knowledge is better equipped to manage the practice issue.

NICOLE

"Ironic, isn't it?" asked Nicole at the end of a meeting with her attorney. "So many times, I was the one who questioned the ethics of other professionals who were working with my clients. Now I find myself accused." It had been a dizzying three days, and Nicole's emotions ranged from embarrassment to anger. In retrospect she could see how her decision to offer services to the Hobart family had been a mistake.

Nicole worked at a local mental health agency as a part-time clinical social worker. Her caseload included an elderly woman, Anna Hobart, who had been diagnosed with depression and who was experiencing increasing confusion.

Hobart's sister and brother-in-law, her only family, grew to trust Nicole, who was caring and seemed to appreciate their difficulty in continuing to care for Anna Hobart in a safe manner.

The family asked Nicole whether anyone could help them to find a skilled nursing facility and to become eligible for benefits, including Medicaid and coverage of prescription drugs, because Anna Hobart's savings were nearly depleted. Nicole provided a list of town services and mentioned that she does that type of work in her private practice as an elder care manager. The family members asked Nicole whether she would help them, and Nicole quickly agreed.

It is difficult not to cringe at Nicole's decision. Providing care to a client in the capacity of clinician while agreeing to serve as a private case manager is an obvious conflict of interest. When she submitted a bill for her first month's services (which were legitimately and competently delivered), a Title 19 eligibility caseworker for the state questioned the size of the bill.

Nicole's subsequent legal troubles included being investigated for billing fraud by the state. The clinic suspended her and referred the case to the state licensing board as well as the Committee on Inquiry of the state chapter of the National Association of Social Workers. She was accused of improper solicitation and exerting undue influence on a vulnerable client.

Was Nicole guilty of a well-intentioned breach, of wanting to help the family but not stopping to think about the consequences? Was she guilty of putting herself first, given that she was paying the bills for her new private practice? A better understanding of the legal implications of ethical violations could have helped Nicole to take more care in designing and following accepted professional standards for her practice. Once the complaint was filed, Nicole encountered the legal system as a *client* in need of representation.

RAUL

Raul had never experienced such an intrusion into his practice. In his twelve years of working for the child guidance clinic, he had avoided as many interactions with the legal system as he could. This time the legal system had forced its way right into his therapeutic relationship with two young sisters, and he felt unprepared to respond.

Sara and Janine, aged seven and nine, respectively, experienced the type of emotional upheaval frequently associated with a contentious divorce. Their

mother brought them in for counseling after seeing a drop in their school performance and hearing the girls express fear about visiting their dad. The children were beginning to do some productive work with Raul when the family
court issued an order that jeopardized the therapy. After hearing testimony in
the custody case about the girls' fear of visiting their father, the judge ordered
that the visits should be supervised. When the father complained of the additional cost, the judge extended the order to require that the supervised visits
take place during the children's therapy sessions with Raul.

Raul's outrage increased when his agency's executive director informed him
that it appeared that nothing could be done, because the court had issued the
order. Raul and his agency colleagues could have responded to the inappropriate court order in a number of ways, but their lack of sophisticated knowledge about the law and the absence of legal representation for the agency created a sense of powerlessness and resigned acceptance.

JULIE

Julie was shocked when her field instructor told her that she would have to find
a new placement. In the first six weeks of the semester Julie had been learning
about the legal system in her practicum with the public defender's office. She had
been working with a lawyer–social worker team that was providing services to
low-income people in the criminal justice system. In every way, she appeared to
be doing well, until a casual conversation over lunch unraveled her world.

Julie's question seemed innocent to her. "How would I handle a case where
a client reported something to me that seemed to be child abuse?" The public
defender blanched and responded that Julie was bound by the lawyers' obligation to attorney-client privilege because she was working as part of a legal
team. "But how do I reconcile that with being a mandated reporter?" The
lawyer stiffened, picked up the rest of his lunch, and said that he would take it
up with her supervisor. Later that afternoon Julie was called into the social
worker's office. Her supervisor told Julie that the attorney felt that she could
no longer be trusted to maintain client confidences, and he was unwilling to
"put his license on the line" for an intern who could not accept the reality of
working in a legal setting.

Julie had not recognized the importance of confidentiality for the public defender. "After all," she later reasoned, "don't social workers have the same
duty to keep client information private and to prevent harm?" The chief social
worker for the public defender's office acknowledged that the staff does not

discuss the issue of mandated reporting because it engenders such strong emotions. She reported that the lawyers see all staff members as part of a legal team and, as such, defer to the attorney to decide as a legal matter whether confidential information can ever be released.

STAFF ADVOCACY

The social work staff at the AIDS service agency was becoming more frustrated each day. For the past three years, the city consistently had cut the budget for the Division of AIDS Services. As a result, caseworker positions were eliminated, while benefits were delayed and reduced. A group of AIDS activists met and decided to file a class action lawsuit on behalf of city residents who had AIDS. The activists asked the social workers to identify clients who had been harmed by the cutbacks, to document their stories, and to determine their willingness to participate in the lawsuit. Eventually, a federal judge ruled that the city had failed to provide adequate services and ordered the agency placed under the oversight of a federal monitor. The social workers, operating as part of an advocacy group, played an important role in filing a legal challenge to the deficient services and helping thousands of clients with a single intervention.

MARTIN

Martin, a licensed clinical social worker, was understandably anxious when he learned that he would have to give a deposition at a large downtown law firm. He had been treating a man who suffered from acute anxiety and stress. The client was suing his employer for allowing a supervisor to harass and intimidate him, allegedly causing the client's symptoms. After receiving notice of the deposition and a phone call from an aggressive attorney, Martin contacted a lawyer with mental health expertise. This attorney met with Martin to educate him about the process of a lawsuit and the purpose of a deposition, the elements of a case that needed to be proved, and the role of his testimony in the case. Finally, the lawyer conducted a mock deposition, helping Martin to formulate his responses to probable questions. Martin went into the deposition with newfound confidence and returned from the deposition in great spirits. He reported to his consulting attorney that his understanding of the process and the elements of the legal case allowed him to stay calm in the face of an intense interrogation and to provide testimony that accurately reflected his work with this client.

THE SOCIAL CONSTRUCTION OF LAWYERS

Some would argue that the mercenary image of lawyers in the 1980s, vividly captured by the television drama *L.A. Law,* led many lawyers to reconsider their priorities and to reject the glitzy, empty lifestyle (Porsdam 1999). The notion of winning at all costs may have had the most severe repercussions for the image and personal satisfaction of practicing lawyers. And the fantastic coverage of the O. J. Simpson trial, which exposed the nature of adversarial litigation and the behavior of lawyers, had influence on the public perception of lawyers that cannot be overstated.

These social experiences enhanced interest in legal reform and established legal movements such as mediation. Many in the legal community, particularly legal educators, began to examine alternative styles of legal practice that focused on securing justice and "good" outcomes for clients rather than merely winning a case. Recent legal reform movements have gained momentum, and law schools are exposing tomorrow's lawyers to ideas in law that would have been impossible just a few years ago.

Some examples of reform include a tremendous increase in the use of mediation and arbitration (alternative dispute resolution); the growing influence of the therapeutic jurisprudence perspective, an area of scholarship that examines the therapeutic and antitherapeutic outcomes of legal actions (Wexler 1990); and the renewed interest in preventive law strategies that keep clients out of court by careful communication and planning by lawyers and systems within a client's environment (Stolle and Wexler 1997). A recent trend that has garnered considerable attention recommends that lawyers encourage their clients to apologize rather than engage in the denials or silence usually recommended to those at risk of being sued (Cohen 1999). These and other reform initiatives bring more lawyers closer to the values and practices of social workers and create opportunities for collaboration. While important, these trends should not be overstated. The reality is that many practicing attorneys remain entrenched in the adversarial, results-focused practice of law.

At the same time the social work field has focused increased attention on the need for practitioners to develop interprofessional skills (Meares 1998). Social workers are recognizing the value of coordinated problem solving with different professions, each with unique knowledge, skills, perspectives, and personal attributes (Andrews 1990). Building bridges between professions enables individuals from different disciplines to reinforce and support each other in meeting clients' needs (Council on Social Work Education 1998). Establishing successful partnerships with legal professionals will require significant improvement in the legal knowledge base of all social workers.

Social work scholars have long understood that the legal system can be an important focus for efforts to change policy (Albert 2002). Whether by influencing legislation, testifying in court cases, providing social science research to the court, or participating in class action suits to enforce the rights of marginalized populations, social workers have an important role to play in legal policy practice (Madden 2000a). In the depths of the Great Depression a Maryland judge, Joseph Ulman, spoke to the National Conference of Social Work and implored social workers to study ways in which the law could be an important instrument in social reform efforts (1933). The renewed interest in developing a foundation of basic legal knowledge for social work practice can help to reinforce this commitment to use the law as a creative force.

LEARNING ABOUT THE LAW

Subsequent chapters will explore the structure of the legal system, the nature of jurisprudence, and the intricacies of legal practice. First, it is important to gain comfort with reading and understanding law as it is written in statutes and cases. Certain structural elements to most statutes and cases enable a reader to cull the key points from what may seem at first to be impenetrable language. Later chapters will deal with how laws develop and change.

READING AND UNDERSTANDING STATUTES

Most statutes and proposed legislation on the state and federal levels have common structural elements. When reading statutory language, breaking the legal rules down into manageable units is important.

All legislation carries a particular numerical designation. Proposed legislation generally has a house bill (HB) or senate bill (SB) prefix, depending on which body originated the measure. A statute has a public law number; once the law takes effect, it will be codified. Sometimes a statute becomes known by its public law number, as was the case with the original special education law, popularly called 94–142. More often, a bill will be referred to by its title (for example, the Adoption and Safe Families Act) or by an acronym, as is the case with the successor special education law called IDEA (Individuals with Disabilities Education Act).

At the beginning of a large, complex statute, the legislature may provide formal findings that state the basis of the law. The findings may also may contain a statement of the purpose of the statute. For example, the privileged communication statute in most state codes appears in the evidence section and states the general intention of the legislation in the initial sentences. Where the language of the statute is more limited and discrete, these preliminary sections may not be included.

The next section is a list of definitions of terms used in the statute to detail what circumstances or conditions the law covers. In the case of privileged communication statutes, the privilege applies only to social workers with a particular license or certification and, in some states, anyone working under the direct supervision of these professionals.

The body of the statute attempts to put the law into a form that carries out the intentions of the legislature. Here the average reader succumbs to the autonomic response of the brain to shut down when faced with impossibly complex and arcane language. It is important to break a statute down by section to understand the whole. An effective technique is to outline who or what the law covers, under what circumstances the law applies, what the exceptions, if any, are, and whether any policies are explicit or implicit in the language of the statute.

The specific content of a statute is often referred to as "the rule of law." Despite the association of the rule of law with clear mandates, determining the parameters of a statute is not always a straightforward process because legislators tend to write in general language to respond to a particular problem or social situation. Several statutes, some of which may conflict, could apply to a single set of facts.

For example, does the privileged communication statute apply to psychotherapy provided to a man accused of a heinous crime? An Alaska court had required a man to attend therapy, which he later voluntarily continued (*State v. Wetherhorn*). The state subsequently attempted to force the psychotherapist to testify in front of a grand jury about statements made by the man, who was accused of child abuse.

This case raises several issues requiring statutory interpretation because the text of the law fails to directly address the following issues: Does the privileged communication statute apply when the court has ordered the treatment? Was the initial period of evaluation presented to the client as confidential, and, if not, should the therapist have given the client an explicit warning of his right not to make self-incriminating statements? Does the law requiring all clinicians to report incidents of child abuse apply when the client has already been arrested and charged with child abuse? Does the mandated reporting statute require a clinician to testify in front of a grand jury?

Analyzing this case would require identifying the social policy considerations of the statutes. Generally, the plain language of the statute has the most weight when a court has been asked to interpret the law. In some cases a judge uses the legislative history to assess the intent of the statute. This might include a review of legislative testimony, legislators' speeches, committee reports, and other documents. In most jurisdictions examining legislative history is complicated and most frequently used by lawyers and judges involved in litigation.

The social worker looking to read and understand the intent of a statute must supplement the reading of the language with a look at cases that have analyzed and applied the law. In doing basic research on statutes, it is helpful to select the *annotated* versions of the statutes (see the appendix for a more complete discussion of legal research). These volumes include a summary of cases that have analyzed the respective sections of the statute.

READING AND UNDERSTANDING CASES

Jurisdictions document case law in a relatively consistent manner. Most published cases come from appellate courts. Although the transcripts and written decisions for most trial court cases are available, reviewing specific issues of law is the purview of the appellate courts. Because the appellate courts address issues of law that might result in new interpretations of statutes, clarification of legal rules, or the application of a law to an evolving area, each jurisdiction publishes the decisions to maintain a record for future use and to let the public know about new developments in the law.

In reading a case, it is important to recognize the components of an opinion. The case name generally lists the plaintiff (person filing the case) first, followed by the defendant (person against whom the action is brought). In some appellate courts, however, the name of the person bringing the appeal (appellant) is listed first. Case names usually are shortened by using last names or the name of a government agency (frequently cited as the name of the administrative head of the agency). Criminal cases usually list the United States (when the case involves an alleged violation of a federal statute) or the state as the plaintiff because it is the party bringing the criminal complaint to court.

Social workers should be aware that court cases are public, and published opinions contain the real names and details of the controversy unless the judge grants a motion to use a pseudonym. Judges in family court and other sensitive, confidential cases can order the names of the parties to be changed to protect their privacy. In many instances courts use a litigant's first name, initials, or a generic term such as "Doe" to identify the case.

Court opinions are published in volumes called reporters. Each jurisdiction maintains official reporters, and private services such as Westlaw and LEXIS-NEXIS compile unofficial reporters and searchable databases. Each case is identified by a citation that lists the volume number, the name of the reporter, including the edition, and the first page of the decision (for example, 349 F. Supp. 1078 (E.D.N.Y. 1968) directs the reader to the *Federal Supplement,* volume 349, page 1078). The citation should include the location of the court (in this case, the federal district court for the Eastern District of New York), followed by the year that the case was decided.

Case opinions list the attorneys representing the parties, the judge or judges hearing the case, and the dates of the hearing and the decision. Depending on the court, the opinion may include a summary of the court's ruling, sometimes referred to as a syllabus. Some decisions list the disposition of a case, which is the technical, procedural directive issued by the court, such as overturning a lower court decision, remanding a case for a new hearing by the trial court on a particular issue, or affirming the decision of a lower court.

The beginning of a case opinion generally identifies the issue being presented on appeal. In some cases the appeal will question whether the trial court used the correct law to decide the case. In other cases the question may be whether the court applied the law correctly. It may be a question concerning whether an individual's constitutional rights were violated. Most legal rules can be broken down into essential elements as spelled out by a statute, through the common law, or through precedents (prior cases). These elements structure the judicial opinion of how the law applies to the specific facts of the case under consideration.

The court opinion describes the legal controversy by reciting the basic facts of the case. Then the opinion provides an analysis of the issues to be decided in the appeal. Many judges will discuss both sides of an argument to illustrate the rationale used in reaching the decision. The court announces its ruling and answers the legal question in the case in a section of the opinion called the holding. Unfortunately, opinions do not always clearly identify the holding, and determining what the court actually held as its legal ruling may be difficult. At times a court may include language about a legal issue not specific to the holding. These statements, called dicta, may be influential in that they suggest how the court might rule on an issue if it comes before it, but a dictum is not binding on future rulings or trial court decisions. The final part of the court opinion directs the outcome of the case, such as finding for the plaintiffs or the defendants, answering a legal question, affirming or reversing a lower court decision, or returning a case to a lower court for retrial in accordance with the legal ruling. In some appellate decisions one or more justices who do not agree with the majority opinion will choose to write a dissent, specifying an alternative view of the legal question. Dissents can be influential because they sometimes set forth a new direction for the law that eventually may be adopted.

Subsequent chapters will discuss the role of precedent in legal reasoning. However, social workers studying the law should be careful not to overreact to individual cases because they rarely set a professional standard. The 1976 *Tarasoff* case may be the rare exception, because it created a new duty (the duty to warn) for mental health professionals. In most cases the holding is narrow, meaning that it applies to the specific set of facts in the case at hand. Common law develops in part from a series of cases, each teasing out an additional strand of the law, giving direction to the interpretation of statutory language.

Cases give specific form to statutes. Statutes are read most effectively in conjunction with the important cases that help define the law. Social workers new to the law must remember that knowledge of legal rules includes an understanding of the policy considerations that influence the ways in which the rule is applied and interpreted. Although legislatures and courts are mindful of the need for predictability in the legal system and tend to follow the precedents of past legal decisions, considerations of politics and values can result in surprising and controversial decisions.

INDUCTIVE REASONING: FROM PRACTICE PROBLEMS TO LEGAL PRINCIPLES

Knowledge of inductive reasoning is basic to the understanding of legal opinions, laws, and regulations. Inductive reasoning is a method of reasoning that moves from the particular to the general. Lawyers and judges use an inductive reasoning process to analyze the grounds that other courts used to decide similar cases, an analysis that yields the general legal principles that consistently underpin those decisions.

Social workers are familiar with finding general rules by studying specific cases. In practice, experience allows for understanding the common dynamics associated with each setting. A social worker in a dialysis unit develops a knowledge base about the range of emotional responses of patients and families. A child therapist recognizes a set of behaviors as consistent with the responses of other children who have been through repetitive trauma and explores the possibility that a child has been abused. Social workers use observation to develop hypotheses that they can test empirically and evaluate against existing research to create theory (Berlin and Marsh 1993).

In the law inductive reasoning follows a similar process. One can study cases and recognize common analyses and results. From these collective outcomes a court can generate a legal rule. When the facts of a case match a certain pattern of cases, we would expect the analysis of the legal issues to proceed in a consistent, predictable manner. The reality is that inductive reasoning may provide an outline of the legal principle, but the facts of a case might result in the creation of an exception to the usual rule.

Social workers seeking to understand the law and its guidance for practice should read numerous cases on a subject to ascertain the legal principles. For example, in the *Tarasoff* case, the California Supreme Court justices identified a number of factual conditions that created the duty to warn. The social worker who reads the case carefully can recognize the essential elements highlighted by the court: a legitimate and serious threat of serious harm, and an identified/identifiable third party who is the intended victim. Other cases have explored the different level of duty required when a client is an inpatient (see, for example, *Fraser v. United States* [1996]). Still others applied a similar framework for preventing harm to suicidal clients (case law summarized in Swenson 1993:188–91) or explored the scope of the duty owed to nonclients such as family members (Madden and Parody 1997).

Social workers who follow developments in case law, within their state and across the country, naturally use an inductive reasoning process. Through a careful comparison of cases and an analysis of the elements of legal rules, a social worker can develop a sophisticated understanding of the current treatment issues and can use this legal knowledge to resolve practice dilemmas.

2.

EXPLORING JURISPRUDENCE: LEGAL PHILOSOPHY

Philosophy is not a body of doctrine but an activity. —Wittgenstein

IN THIS CHAPTER I will examine the basic schools of thought in the law and will argue that many legal decisions occur because of personal values and underlying principles that often are unexpressed. In exploring the philosophy of law, I will focus on how values and principles derive from beliefs about the role of government and the place of legal rules in society. Many treatises identify a school of legal thought or legal philosophy to explain the way that our legal system operates—or should operate. Students of the law need to understand the basic schools of legal thinking. However, discerning how legal theory affects the daily practice of the law is difficult. The essence of the law is not to be found in books but in the everyday interactions of judges, lawyers, and citizens (Feinman 2000).

Legislatures divided by political ideology enact laws that more often reflect compromise than a unified philosophical position. The resulting statutes may express policy preferences but often articulate the law in vague or incomplete language that emerges from the political process. Judges are expected to decide difficult cases at the edges of legal rules in order to reach just outcomes for the litigants and for society. In theory a principled decision consistent with a philosophical view is desirable. In practice, however, few judges are also philosophers (Sunstein 1996). If legal professionals do not use a manifest philosophical approach, do some discoverable underlying principles guide their routine legal thinking and decision making?

Legal reasoning today belongs to no particular philosophical school but rather is a patchwork of ideas from various intellectual traditions (Vandevelde 1998). Individuals may harbor strongly held beliefs that influence the way that they look at a legal duty, but often people often use a philosophical rationale as a pretext for making a political decision. Understanding this dynamic will help social workers to participate in the process and influence legal decisions.

A socialization process that requires a level of rigor, respect, and consistency with existing law restrains the behavior of judges and lawyers. Law school education and professional socialization instill a strong taboo against being unprepared. The competitive, adversarial nature of most legal procedures helps to reinforce the practice of doing one's homework, or research, before any hearing. The rules of courts and the sanctions against those who violate them ensure that lawyers demonstrate respect and deference to the judges, even when they vigorously disagree. Because of the societal need for predictability of the law, legal actors must follow a rational process for seeking changes in it. By its very nature, our legal system is conservative and change is incremental, thus reinforcing consistency in the system.

In the social work literature Maroney (1991) has argued that values shape the creation and analysis of social policies. If we think about the law as an expression of society's values and legal reasoning as an exercise in policy analysis, we can deconstruct the first principles (underlying values and beliefs) in a piece of legislation or a judicial decision. While the schools of legal thought may not prove to be enlightening to a social worker in the abstract, understanding this theoretical material is the basic tool for analyzing the law.

The manner in which dispute resolution and legal decision making occur reflects the underlying philosophical beliefs and political ideologies of the actors in the legal system. Every day judges must select among alternative outcomes in cases before them. Should they rely on the letter of the law to find the legal rule that controls the case? Should they look to the outcomes to assess the most morally supportable result? Should they look to the possibility that they can improve some aspect of society by finding a new right or duty that had not previously been codified? Understanding the underpinnings of the legal system—the historical and philosophical views of the law and the styles of judicial decision making that flow from each—allows social workers to communicate more effectively with legal professionals and be more effective as advocates for a more therapeutic legal system.

NATURALISM

Most examinations of natural law focus on the writings of Saint Thomas Aquinas. Aquinas began with some assumptions about human existence. He believed that human existence has a certain order and purpose. That purpose is to achieve happiness. He further believed that he could ascertain the natural laws by observing the basic laws of nature and the interactions among people that result in maximum happiness. Aquinas set down conditions for developing laws. First, a law is a rule that induces people to act or to refrain from certain actions. For Aquinas, reason determines the ends, which must conform to natural law. Every law must support and enhance the common good and should be made by those who have been assigned responsibility to care for all the people. Finally, because the law affects the whole population, people need to know the law. It must be promulgated or published so that people know the rules (Aquinas [1266–72] 1945).

For Aquinas, the basis of natural laws was the perceived will of God, as articulated in the Scriptures. The Scriptures presented humans as having been created in the image and likeness of God and thus, by extension, naturally given to moral and rational behavior. Aquinas believed that all human laws have to be consistent with natural law and divine law (Samar 1998).

A shift in the perceived source of natural laws began to develop during the Enlightenment period of the late 1600s through the late 1700s. During this time scholars promoted the value of reasoning and scientific inquiry as methods that could bring people to new ways of knowing. In the American colonies Enlightenment thinkers profoundly influenced political (democratic) and economic (capitalist) thinking.

The Enlightenment produced thinkers such as Isaac Newton, who developed the laws of physics. The idea people could find rules to explain observable phenomena scientifically reinforced the notion of a rational system of discoverable truths by which the natural world operates. The existence of laws of nature supported the idea that human nature has analogous laws. The extension of this reasoning gave rise to liberal political theory, perhaps best articulated by John Locke, whose social contract theory postulates that all humans have a natural right to liberty and equality. Governments represent a form of agreement made by all humans to protect these natural rights. These and other prominent political, economic, scientific, and philosophical traditions influenced the construction of the American political and legal systems, including the Constitution and the subsequent codification of the Bill of Rights.

Such a rational description of the law provides a great deal of comfort, at least at first. For example, an examination of nature will yield the principle of self-preservation. Using this principle to view human interactions might suggest laws against murder or laws that support peaceful coexistence. Natural law regards morality as consistent with the best interests of society, and it therefore creates universal rules or guidelines for living. In Aquinas's view the natural laws came directly from Christian religious tradition. The Enlightenment produced an alternative view, that reason and observation of nature could find the source of natural laws. Through science and reason, natural law had acquired a secular character (Vandevelde 1998).

In the early years of American law, belief in natural law was deeply ingrained. The words of the first legal documents of the new nation reflect this: "We hold these Truths to be self-evident; that all Men are created equal, that they are endowed by their Creator with certain unalienable Rights." The design of the government, with separation of the legislative, administrative, and judicial branches, further reflects the rational thinking about how to protect liberty and other essential rights. By applying reason, one could determine the natural laws, including the protection of life, liberty, and the pursuit of happiness.

The American view of natural rights was not without its critics. Jeremy Bentham, for example, found the idea of unalienable rights problematic. Bentham was a utilitarian, believing that society should be designed in a way that results in the greatest good for the greatest number of people. The existence of individual rights led to the conclusion that if a law impinged on an individual right, rejecting it was justifiable. Bentham saw this as a recipe for revolution, citing the American and French Revolutions as examples of a small group of citizens that was rejecting the legitimacy of existing governments. Bentham argued that an individual right should be protected only if it benefits the whole of society.

The religious form of natural law contains the idea that all modern law is invalid if it conflicts with natural or divine law. This orientation underscores the political rhetoric that characterizes the religious right today, but it is not the only vestige of natural law theory. Those who use moral judgments to decide abstract or vague laws, or constitutional principles, are using a modern application of natural law (Dworkin 1996). Both liberals and conservatives do this. Although natural law has a limited role in current jurisprudential debate, one could argue that natural law continues to exert a powerful force on judicial decision making. Judges apply their own moral positions, frequently based on personal or religious beliefs, to decide cases involving controversial social issues.

For example, in the debate about abortion the Supreme Court's liberal justices, giving priority to the first principle of freedom (stated more specifically as a privacy right), implicitly took the moral position that the Constitution should be read as supporting a woman's right to choose whether to have an abortion. However, conservative legal thinkers have used the first principle of equality to support the moral position of the right of a fetus to possess the same right to life as any person in U.S. society. What is important in the analysis of contemporary legal decisions is the identification of a moral rationale.

A law that derives its legitimacy from a moral position can be powerful. Often statutes or previous cases do not cover a specific situation. A judge applying the law may need to reach for the underlying moral principle to decide a case correctly. The majority of the judiciary in the United States share a Judeo-Christian heritage that sometimes results in a narrow view of what is moral and natural.

LEGAL POSITIVISM

Legal positivism is a generic term that has had many forms. It is most commonly associated with the idea that the law consists of those legal rules, statutes, and cases that a government entity or a court has established. A key element of legal positivism is a rejection of the natural law premise that the law must be connected with morality. In fact, positivism accepts that a legal rule may exist even where it is inconsistent with moral principles. As such, a judge applying the law from a positivist tradition would seek to understand the law as the legislature intended or as consistent with existing case law in situations where no statute is controlling.

John Austin, writing in the 1870s, saw three conditions for a rule to be valid under the theory of positive law. First, the rule had to be expressed as a command to the people in society, issued for a specific purpose, and backed by the power to sanction violations. Second, a sovereign power had to issue the command. Finally, the society for which the rule is issued must be an independent political society (1873).

In the contemporary positivist view, H. L. A. Hart has amended Austin's theory by stipulating that the acceptance of positive laws occurs when the citizenry accepts the law, not out of fear or coercion—as Austin's command approach suggests—but because it feels that the law represents a legitimate exercise of sovereign power that followed proper procedure (1983). This reflects Hart's concern that Austin's style of positivism was similar to the legal systems developed by fascist governments in Germany and Italy in the 1930s in which the judiciary was not autonomous. If the only criteria used to determine the legitimacy of a law is a technically appropriate exercise of sovereign power, Hart believes, the potential exists for political power to usurp legal authority. As a result, Hart argues that judges should decide cases in which no legal rule is controlling by linking their decisions to established legal principles in analogous decisions or laws.

The primary criticism of a positivist perspective on the law is that it can result in a mechanical process of judicial decision making. According to the critics, the use of logic—deducing correct decisions from clearly articulated legal rules—resulted in a largely fictitious process. It ignored the indeterminacy of statutes and constitutional provisions. As a result, the critics contend that when judges must choose which legal rule to apply to a specific set of facts, they must look to social policies and values (Hart 1983). In doing so, they are creating law, something that legal positivism seems to expressly reject.

SCHOOLS OF LEGAL THOUGHT

Natural law and legal positivism are the primary sources of American law, embodying the historic, cultural, and moral foundations of the United States. From these two legal traditions a number of schools of legal thought have emerged that attempt to explain the process of legal reasoning. These schools of legal thought include legal formalism, legal realism, several branches of each of these major schools, as well as critical legal schools of thought that seek to lay bare the underlying power dynamics of the legal system. Throughout the chapter I will use the case that follows to illustrate the way that legal professionals can be guided by the values and principles associated with legal movements to reach different legal conclusions:

A sixteen-year-old gave birth to a baby girl. In the hospital she told the social worker that she wished to give the child up for adoption. The social worker called the state child welfare office, which sent a caseworker to interview the girl. Believing that the young woman was a troubled youth with minimal family support, the caseworker encouraged her to sign papers for the adoption. The caseworker did not respond to calls from the girl during the next several days and inappropriately pushed the paperwork through the process. The infant was placed with an adoptive family that had been waiting years for a child.

Once released from the hospital, the birth mother lived in various locations, including a series of shelters. She received no notice of the hearings held in the adoption process because the worker had no address or telephone number for her. The birth mother called the caseworker three times during the six months following the birth but never was able to reach him. She left no numbers or addresses because of her uncertain living conditions.

Two months after the final adoption the birth mother spoke to a lawyer who was doing volunteer work at the shelter. She explained what little she knew about the adoption process and expressed her desire to have her child returned to her. State law was silent on the time limit for appealing a final adoption, but the rules of the family court set a deadline of forty-five days for such an appeal. Although unable to contact the biological mother directly, the state followed the technical requirements of providing notice by attempting to locate her at her last known address and by publishing the adoption notice in the legal notices section of the local newspapers.

The biological mother's attorney argued that because her client's due process rights were violated, especially in regard to the lack of notice about the legal hearings and time lines, and because the caseworker's actions were contrary to professional standards, the court should overturn the adoption and return the child to her biological mother. The adoptive parents argued that they were the child's psychological parents, having nurtured her for seven of the nine months since her birth. Further, they cited their economic stability and suburban home as a superior environment in which to raise a child, especially when compared to the biological mother's limited resources and uncertain living conditions.

LEGAL FORMALISM

Christopher Columbus Langdell, writing in the latter part of the nineteenth century, suggested that law is a science and, as such, its truths can be figured out by studying printed books. Langdell believed that the law is embodied in the plain meaning of the language in established cases and statutes and in scholarly treatises on legal doctrines. This approach, known as legal formalism, posits that the careful study of these sources can result in a limited number of fundamental legal rules applicable to all cases (Langdell 1871). Legal positivism has an authoritarian element, that is, obedience to the text.

Formalism emerged from the positivist school and is consistent with the basic principles of legal positivism—a system of rules that a judge is bound to apply (Berns 1993). Legal reasoning is considered a deductive process, starting from legal premises that are accepted as true. The analytic process is strict, and the goal is to analyze many judicial opinions related to the legal issue in order to uncover the underlying principle. This view posits that law can be objective. The judge must apply the principle to the facts to decide the case in question. The primary question for the judge, then, is what is the law? What the law *should be* remains a political question, to be determined through democratic procedures such as the legislative process.

The formalist view of the law corresponded to the emerging ideals of empiricism and the scientific revolution. A formalist outlook on the world assumes that through rigorous, fact-based research, one can determine truths about life and society. Formalism also has roots in laissez-faire economics and social Darwinism. The first principle underlying formalism is freedom. Formalist scholars believed that courts should not interfere with the natural processes of society, whether that is the economic system or the establishment of civil rights laws.

A problem with strict formalism involves the limits of language and emerging issues in U.S. society. Judges often face gaps or inconsistencies between a legal principle and a set of facts. They would seem to need a normative theory, a set of underlying values, to guide their decisions. The notion that the objective answer always can be found in an existing legal principle left no room for consideration of justice or fairness in deciding cases. By the early years of the twentieth century, critics were increasingly skeptical about the formalism school, questioning whether it could provide an intellectually supportable system of legal reasoning.

A judge deciding the contested adoption case from a formalist perspective might reason in the following way. It is important to look to the text of the law to determine the deadlines for filing an appeal to contest an adoption. Although the statute is silent on this issue, past court practice and the explicit time limit in the published rules of the family court make it clear that the forty-five-day limit is controlling. A judge who is a legal formalist would not be inclined to examine the underlying facts, because the state met the technical requirements of notice; nothing in the letter of the law supports reopening the adoption. A formalist analysis would result in a ruling in favor of keeping the child with the adoptive parents.

The acknowledged critical moment in legal history that spurred the decline of legal formalism and the movement toward legal realism was the famous case of *Lochner v. New York* (1905). *Lochner* involved a New York state law that attempted to regulate the maximum number of hours that bakers could be required to work. The U.S. Supreme Court struck down this law, basing its analysis on the underlying principle of freedom of contract. Using a formalist reasoning process, the Court held that a law limiting the opportunity of the bakers to freely contract for whatever number of hours they wished violated freedom of contract. Justice Oliver Wendell Holmes, in one of the most famous and influential dissents in U.S. legal history, blasted the formalist notion of fundamental legal principles by writing that "general propositions do not decide concrete cases." Holmes identified the unequal bargaining power of the bakers and the owners and deferred to the reasonableness of the state legislature, which had recognized the need for such legislation to prevent abuses.

Lochner shows that formalism contains an inherent tendency to support economic and political power by treating all people the same, without reference to social, historical, political, or economic factors. The development of the legal realist movement began the process of moving away from the deductive "science" developed by Langdell and toward the more socially conscious empirical approach used by legal realists (Vandevelde 1998).

LEGAL REALISM

It is revolting to have no better reason for a rule of law than that so it was laid down in the time of Henry IV. It is still more revolting if the grounds upon which it was laid down have vanished long since, and the rule simply persists from blind imitation of the past.   —Oliver Wendell Holmes

The influential Holmes argued that most cases present difficult questions involving a balancing of rights. Holmes saw laws as the rules of a community that govern the behavior of its members. His maxim, "the law is what the courts say it is," summarizes the legal realist's retort to the mechanical jurisprudence and deductive reasoning of formalism. Like all these legal philosophies, several subgroups of legal realism have developed over time.

Roscoe Pound, one of the earliest to react against formalism, promulgated a school of thought that he termed social jurisprudence, which emphasized the emerging role of law to address social needs (1911). Pound believed that lawyers and judges could act as social engineers, fashioning decisions in legal cases to achieve positive social purposes. To place this in historical context, most of Pound's publications appeared during the Progressive Era when Americans were developing many proposals for reforming social institutions. As with other Progressive Era reform proposals, Pound's ideas were perhaps too radical for his time, the early 1900s. However, they influenced Holmes and the overall development of legal realism's empirical foundations.

This new perspective required that legal thinkers be literate in a variety of subjects in addition to the traditional positivist study of authoritative legal sources (Posner 1990). This change in legal philosophy made possible the integration of the social sciences, such as economics, sociology, anthropology, and psychology, into the study and practice of law.

The legal realism approach views the function and purpose of a judge as not merely to apply the law to a set of facts but to be a community problem solver by deciding controversies (Samar 1998). The legal realists rejected the idea that the law was merely a system of rules. In their criticism of formalists legal realists complained that when a rule did not fit a set of facts, judges often decided cases in line with their personal views but then created a pretext for the decision by claiming a basis in established law. Legal realists acknowledged that in the real world, judges had much discretion in deciding cases. When the text does not provide the answer, the judge must exercise discretion to make law. Legal realists believed that in resolving difficult cases judges ought to be guided by instincts informed by empirical data.

Taken to its extreme, legal realism could be seen as supporting the proposition that there is no government of laws, only a government of men (Murphy and Coleman 1990). It is important to understand that legal realism was a reaction to the injustices and elitism of formalists. As such, it can best be thought of as a critical school rather than one that postulates a coherent legal philosophy.

The legal realists were able to introduce discussion of the actual practice of law and the process of adjudication that went beyond the academic exercises of previous legal theories. The application of rules clearly had a place in legal realist thought. Holmes himself acknowledged that "law is a prediction of what courts will decide." A judge's discretion becomes most evident in the difficult cases, where the law is unclear, where the facts do not fit the language of the law, or where no written rule exists. Legal realists urged social science researchers to develop empirical data on the outcomes of laws. They worked for legislative reforms that would clarify common law rules based on scientific studies of how these rules work in practice (Vandevelde 1998).

The evolution of legal realism produced some legal traditions that minimized the frequency with which judges exercised their discretion and helped to maintain consistency in legal results. The most important of these traditions is judicial restraint, the rule that judges should decide cases on the narrowest question possible. In other words, if a case raises a constitutional issue but also involves a question of how to interpret a local ordinance, a judge should abstain from deciding the constitutional issue if interpreting the statute would resolve the case. Other traditions minimizing judicial discretion include a strict adherence to procedural due process; deference to legislative statements of the law, judicial oversight, and evaluation procedures; and increased public access to the courts through media coverage.

The legal realism movement was enormously influential but may be most important for the questions that it raised about the practice of law. The attempts to empirically determine the proper outcome in a case produced few tangible results. Legal realism has not proved to be a theory that can guide legal thinking. In its critique of formalism and the development of a more pragmatic response to judicial decision making, legal realism moved jurisprudence into contemporary times.

A legal realist might approach the contested adoption case with a broader view of the issues than the formalist would. The legal realist recognizes that judges may use discretion to decide difficult cases. The facts of this case give rise to a number of issues. First, did the actions of the caseworker and the state child welfare agency violate professional standards and preclude the biological mother from giving an informed consent for the baby to be adopted? Did the lack of a diligent effort to find the biological mother constitute a violation of her constitutional rights of due process, specifically the right to receive notice and the right to be heard by the court? Does the silence of the statute on time lines preclude the family court from establishing a deadline for appeals? What is the empirical research on psychological bonding? These and other areas of inquiry might be part of a legal realist's analysis of the case.

Several important movements in legal thinking have emerged since the early 1970s. Although there are other schools of legal thought, three general movements provide an overview of the influences on contemporary legal thinking.

LAW AND ECONOMICS

The primary goal for proponents of law and economics is economic efficiency. Posner (1992) suggests that individuals are pragmatists who decide on a course of action by examining the anticipated benefits or costs associated with each possible course of action. In deciding social policies, the economic approach seeks to analyze which legal rules would lead to the most efficient use of economic resources. Individuals would follow those policies because they would be rational choices, given their economic basis.

Posner believes that judges are uniquely receptive to social sciences such as economics because the legislative or policy-making approach is part of the role that U.S. judges assume (1996:42). This view of the law can be seen as an extension of the legal realism efforts to apply empirical studies to legal reasoning. Law and economics thus tend to be instrumental, seeking to control human behavior by selecting legal rules that maximize economic efficiency.

Focusing on law and economics maximizes economic goals but tends to do so at the cost of the rights and interests of the individual. An orientation of this sort probably results in conservative decisions that protect the interests of established markets and industries. This orientation is unlikely to result in legal rules that support the social justice goals familiar to social workers.

In the contested adoption case a judge with an economic orientation might look at the ability of the two parties to provide for the care of the child. Reasoning that a return of the child to the biological mother would result in an increased likelihood of the child's needing social service benefits, the judge might refuse to reopen the case. Further, if the court opened up adoptions after final court action, the precedent might discourage some couples from seeking adoptions. A child who is adopted becomes the economic and social responsibility of the adoptive parents, while a child who remains in the custody of the state would need to be supported by state-financed programs such as foster care or residential treatment programs. The economic cost of such a result would be influential to the judge who follows the law and economics school.

Some have criticized the economic assumptions in the law and economics school, specifically questioning whether maximizing wealth is a legitimate social goal and whether applying economic analysis to a legal rule is legitimate. Posner has leveled a similar criticism at legal realism and formalism, arguing that these types of legal reasoning lead to interpretations that are "as much creation as discovery" (1996:435). Posner postulates that economic theory can provide an objective basis for a judge's decision and thus would be more legitimate than applying a strict reading of the text.

The most recent scholarship developing from the field of law and economics comes from a group of researchers who are studying human judgment and choice empirically (Rachlinski 2000). These scholars, primarily psychologists, refer to this field as behavioral decision theory (BDT). Their research questions the rational choice concept central to law and economics by studying cognitive processes involved in decision making. BDT represents a step in the effort begun by the legal realists to imbue legal rules with empirical evidence. At this stage the studies primarily question economic assumptions. Increasingly, scholars are applying BDT to broader issues such as jury decision making, contracts, and legal rules related to special populations such as those with mental illness.

Some legal theorists evaluate judicial decisions and the overall role of the government from the perspective of enhancing a particular moral principle. Proponents of rights theories prioritize a human right, liberty or equality, for example, and support government policies and court rulings that advance the right while arguing against actions that diminish the right. This type of focused and principled analysis enables judges and academics to decide diverse cases consistently. A rights perspective creates a legal position that is not bound by formal legal language and tradition but can evolve with changing social conditions.

Ronald Dworkin is the best-known rights theorist. He writes about liberal political philosophy and espouses equality as the most central value to be protected. In Dworkin's view the main purpose of government is to ensure the equal treatment of all people, enabling each individual to have those liberties and resources necessary for equal opportunity in social interactions. When evaluating legal controversies, Dworkin applies the test of equality to argue for a particular outcome.

Rights theory postulates that the normative foundation underlying judicial decisions is moral theory. Just as Dworkin prioritizes equality, many judges base their decisions on a compelling moral conviction concerning another fundamental right. Dworkin suggests that judges give other superficial reasons in deciding difficult cases, such as the intent of the legislature or the words used by the framers of the Constitution. However, what actually drives the legal analyses of these judges is their moral belief system (which may be politically influenced).

Consider the example of a judge who gives top priority to the principles of freedom. The value of freedom is generally a conservative orientation that favors limits on the scope and power of the government and the policies that will impinge least on the free marketplace. This approach supports the liberty of individuals to be free from interference in the form of taxation, unnecessary rules, or other restrictions. However, the same judge may value freedom of speech most highly of all. The judge might then rule in support of the right of the Ku Klux Klan to march in a black neighborhood or of a demonstrator to burn an American flag, even though the ruling would seem to be at odds with a conservative political orientation. This process explains why some justices, when they reach the Supreme Court, will at times vote in ways that seem to be contrary to their former ideological positions. Dworkin has argued that only a moral reasoning process can explain these decisions (1996).

Dworkin uses this rights theory to justify what has been called judicial activism. He claims that it is consistent with the idea of a political democracy and the rule of law. The decisions of "activist judges" are interpretations of text that state broad moral positions or values. Dworkin (1986) suggests that this reliance on morality is not simply a personal preference regarding what constitutes an objective moral position. Instead, he adds the criterion of integrity of the law.

Dworkin describes a number of legal standards that ensure integrity of the law. Regardless of an individual judge's strongly held moral belief, a decision must be reasonably consistent with case law and political practice in the United States. In those "hard cases," where clear statutory language does not exist or that offer a legitimate choice between different positions, a judge should select the legal doctrine that maximizes a moral principle. The political responsibility expected of judges requires them to reach conclusions that they can justify with a moral theory or principle. Further, political legitimacy requires that judges have used the principle to justify previous decisions. This basic premise allows many judges who rule independently to put together a coherent scheme of law.

Dworkin addresses the criticism that a principle could be used as a pretense for a decision by adding the requirement that a judge should decide all cases with a "principled consistency," giving full value to that principle consistently when ruling in other cases. When judgments do not meet this standard of integrity, Dworkin warns that they become ordinary politics in disguise (1996:411). The idea of integrity allows citizens to perceive the law as coherent and structured. Citizens can rely on the integrity of the law and tolerate developmental changes in it only if they see the process as "government by ideal" (Dworkin 1996:83).

Legal rights theorists present their use of deductive reasoning to reach moral principles as a rational process and a search for shared conceptions of what is right and what is just. In American society, which cannot agree about political morality, relying on first principles to ground legal decisions helps to maintain the political legitimacy of the legal system. Dworkin argues that the concept of legitimacy enables the public to accept court decisions, even when a portion of the population disagrees. He characterizes this as "united in community though divided in project interest and conviction" (1996:413).

It is difficult to predict how a "rights theory" judge would rule on the contested adoption case. It would depend on the first principles that guide that judge's rulings. One could argue that no controlling statutory or case law requires a certain result. It would be important for the judge to analyze the legal principles related to each party's claims. The biological mother is arguing that the failure of the state to provide her with competent services was unjust and that the lack of effective notice violated her rights to due process. The state is arguing that it technically followed the legal rules and that allowing finalized adoptions to be overturned would be harmful to public policy. The adoptive parents are arguing that the child has come to bond with them as psychological parents and that the best interests of the child require that she remain with them. All these claims state important legal principles that could be supported with reference to moral positions. It would be crucial to the integrity of the decision for the judge to apply the first principle that is consistent with the judge's previous decisions.

THE CRITICAL SCHOOLS

The law often is presented as being above politics and biases, resolving disputes objectively by applying legal rules and principles. The legal realism movement questioned the legitimacy and coherence of these assumptions and provided the basis for an emerging body of legal scholarship.

The generic term for this school, *critical legal studies,* includes several distinct movements with the common goal of challenging existing systems of power (Albert 2000). Some proponents of critical legal studies borrow heavily from literary criticism, deconstructing the language of the law. An important critical movement has been the work of feminist legal scholars, who have challenged the legal system to change, both in terms of the way the legal system operates and in substantive legal principles such as sexual harassment, domestic violence, and other topics that historically have ignored women's voices.

The philosophical basis for the critical legal studies movement is postmodernism, a movement that has raised questions about the objective legitimacy and truths of scientific, empirical, and professional knowledge. In the process of gaining status and power, the professions, including law and social work, have developed theories and methods that are accepted as truth. Critical legal theorists argue that the knowledge presented as truth is, in reality, contingent on historically specific, cultural constructions. Central to this position is the idea that these constructed truths perpetuate existing power and entrenched political systems.

Critical legal studies scholars focus on uncovering the culturally defined biases and preferences of the law. They expose socially constructed rules as political because they reinforce the power and influence of those in power. The critical legal studies movement rejects the traditional legal notions that a legal conclusion can be arrived at legitimately with either reason or observation. Many scholars of this movement study the use of language in the law. A distrust of legal text leads critical legal theorists to deconstruct the narratives of judicial decisions. Amsterdam and Bruner, for example, have deconstructed several Supreme Court decisions and suggest that the way that justices tell the story of a case and the manner in which they categorize the issues reflect the decision makers' cultural biases (2000).

An important point made by critical legal studies is that these ideological choices are hidden and thus seldom debated. A judge presents the outcome of a case as a logical deduction, inevitably following the rule of law. The only facts that the judge deems relevant are those that support the judge's preferred outcome. According to the critical legal theorists, the legal system preserves social order by deftly feigning legitimacy. In direct contrast to Dworkin's rights theory, critical legal studies rejects the possibility that statutes, cases, and accepted legal principles constitute a coherent moral order.

A recurring criticism of critical legal studies is the charge that the focus of the scholarship is to delegitimize the legal system without offering any ideas for reform. In part, this has occurred because critical legal studies has been primarily an academic movement that has not had a corresponding approach in legal practice (Vandevelde 1998). Just as significantly, developing an approach to jurisprudence while rejecting the legitimacy of knowledge and theory is challenging. Because this field is located in the legal academy, many practicing lawyers have been exposed to these concepts during law school and may subscribe to these ideas. However, in the day-to-day practice of the law the critical legal studies movement has limited practical influence, although it may support an advocacy role in fighting the abuse of legal power and authority.

A number of issues in the contested adoption case would draw the attention of a judge who had been influenced by critical legal studies. First, the judge would scrutinize the concept of terminating the rights of a biological parent, in effect ending the relationship legally. The judge could regard the adoption as nothing more than fiction, supported by the narrative of the child welfare system that children are better off if they are raised in a wealthy, suburban two-parent household than by a poor single mother. Does the signing of a paper by a judge change the actual relationship between the biological mother and child? Does the adoption process articulate systemic class discrimination and result in the purchase of poor children by the wealthy? A judge who is attuned to a critical legal analysis might ask these and other questions that would challenge the legitimacy and truth of existing legal rules and principles.

RECENT LEGAL REFORM MOVEMENTS

Our system is too costly, too painful, too destructive, too inefficient for a truly civilized people.   —Warren Burger

Problems inherent in the legal system have gained growing recognition since the early 1970s. Recent legal reform movements have emerged to provide alternative procedures, perspectives, and practice approaches to the traditional, formal, adversarial contests. The challenge for the legal community is to integrate new practices that reduce the harmful effects that clients experience when they become involved in the legal system while not sacrificing important rights or strategic advantages that clients might have in traditional legal proceedings.

ALTERNATIVE DISPUTE RESOLUTION

Alternative dispute resolution (ADR) is the generic term for a group of problem-solving approaches (primarily mediation and arbitration) for resolving conflicts by means other than litigation. Popular myth would support the idea that most lawyers encourage excessive litigation; no doubt, in some cases that stereotype is accurate. Most attorneys, however, dread those cases in which a client repeatedly calls with instructions to fight each and every point in a conflict. These cases prove to be an unfulfilling way to practice law. In addition, in many cases the client is unable to pay for all the time that the lawyer has put into a chronic, recurring litigation. Lawyers have supported the development of ADR approaches, particularly in those cases in which time or money is a crucial consideration, or where the issues involve ongoing relationships, for which the adversarial process is not desirable. However, because of concern about the potential for losing legal protections, lawyers often have mixed emotions about using alternative processes (Riskin and Westbrook 1998).

In emotional conflicts such as contested custody disputes, the participants can sometimes engage in serial litigation, acting out their anger through repeated motions and hearings that prolong and exacerbate the trauma of the experience. In family and community contexts, nonlawyers, including social workers, have created a variety of dispute resolution forums that may reduce the role of lawyers. In other cases courts have established ADR programs on their own or through the impetus of legislation. For example, Congress passed the Civil Justice Reform Act in 1990, requiring all federal district courts to develop a plan to reduce costs and delays in civil litigation. ADR is one case management principle that the statute recommends.

ADR strategies, especially mediation and arbitration, have increased incrementally in each decade since the 1970s. The use of ADR has grown for three primary reasons. First, as society has become more litigious, courts have developed backlogs of cases that may take years to come to trial. If a person has been injured in a car accident, waiting five years for an insurance company to pay a damage award is burdensome. Both courts and trial attorneys have been supportive of various forms of ADR to reduce the time that it takes to resolve cases. Second, ADR strategies are generally much less expensive than litigation, so the cost savings accrue to both parties in a conflict. Also, ADR methods can calm a conflict, reducing the emotional harm attendant to adversarial litigation.

Some ADR methods are more like judicial processes than others. These adjudication-like methods include arbitration, where parties agree to submit their dispute to a neutral person or panel that they have selected to make a decision. In an arbitration hearing each side ordinarily submits evidence, and the arbitrator (frequently a panel of three selected by some agreed-upon process) decides in favor of one side or the other (Riskin and Westbrook 1998). Some courts require that certain classes of cases proceed initially to arbitration, although either party may seek to return to the court for a trial. Some labor and commercial contracts require submission of any dispute to binding arbitration. Most states and the federal government have statutes that govern the validity and enforcement of arbitration decisions.

Mediation is a consensual form of ADR in which the parties agree to allow an impartial third party help them to resolve a dispute, although the mediator does not have the power to impose a solution or give legal advice. The mediation process has no true binding authority, but an agreement reached in mediation is sometimes enforceable as a contract, depending on the nature of the promises made (Riskin and Westbrook 1998). Some courts require the parties to try mediation before litigation; however, by its very nature mediation calls for voluntary participation. Despite this, mediation is the primary ADR process that the federal district courts use (Plapinger and Stienstra 1996).

One specific type of ADR strategy developed for family court is collaborative law. Each party to a divorce retains a lawyer trained in collaborative law. The role of these lawyers is limited to helping the parties work out an agreement that meets the needs of all. If the collaborative process fails, neither attorney can represent the party any further. The benefits of this approach are the opportunity for negotiation with legal advice and the assurance that one side is not being victimized by having less power in the process. The collaborative law process encourages attorneys to work with their clients in reducing conflict to ensure that the experience remains positive and productive (Nurse and Thompson 1999).

Social workers are well prepared to develop mediation-based ADR programs because these require skills familiar to social workers. In addition, these approaches are more responsive to the needs of many client groups than are traditional legal forums. For example, dispute resolution programs offer great potential for assisting older people and people with disabilities. The American Bar Association Commission on the Legal Problems of the Elderly (2000) identified a number of situations in which ADR approaches would be appropriate, including intergenerational disputes about health-care decision making, guardianship, and estate planning; disputes in subsidized housing complexes and nursing care facilities; managed-care conflicts; and landlord-tenant disputes (2000).

Other creative processes that serve as alternatives to litigation include various types of negotiation, the use of neutral parties to evaluate the strengths and weaknesses of each side's case, and staging minitrials that provide insight into how a real jury might rule (Riskin and Westbrook 1998). Given the tendency of courts and communities nationwide to institutionalize ADR processes, ADR strategies stressing cooperation and coordination will flourish where they are more effective than the adversarial approach for solving complex problems and enhancing public health (Nelson 2000). Social workers have the opportunity to direct clients into such programs and to push for the establishment of alternative dispute resolution programs, both in the courts and in the community.

THERAPEUTIC JURISPRUDENCE

Recently, a new perspective for studying the effects of the law, therapeutic jurisprudence, has gained significant attention. Therapeutic jurisprudence originated in the work of legal scholars concerned about the practice of mental health law. This perspective focuses on the therapeutic and antitherapeutic consequences of laws, legal rules, and legal actors. Therapeutic jurisprudence provides a framework for assessing legal issues, applying social science research to legal questions, and structuring interventions within the legal environment (Madden and Wayne in press). Some legal scholars have examined the consequences of legal rules and have sought to influence the law to further a social policy agenda. Therapeutic jurisprudence is a different type of approach.

David B. Wexler first used of the term *therapeutic jurisprudence* in a paper for the National Institute of Mental Health in 1987. He defined the phrase as "the study of the role of the law itself as a therapeutic agent. Growing out of its origins in mental health law, it is not an end unto itself, but rather an interdisciplinary enterprise designed to produce scholarship that is particularly useful for law reform" (quoted in Schma 1997:81). The early writings on therapeutic jurisprudence concentrated on legal reform, specifically in the mental health arena, but in recent years this perspective has been instrumental in generating research into the effects of legal processes and in developing therapeutic processes in a variety of legal settings.

Rather than beginning with a particular political agenda, such as liberalism, a therapeutic jurisprudence perspective generates inquiries into the effects on a person, family, or community of participating in the legal system. At the heart of therapeutic jurisprudence is the concept that law, consistent with justice, due process, and other relevant normative values, can and should function as a therapeutic agent (Wexler and Winick 1996). Why should society accept as necessary the damage done by adversarial custody battles? What does the research say about the best practices for helping a person addicted to drugs return to a productive lifestyle? Does the current legal system reflect this research and result in outcomes that benefit participants and society as a whole?

As therapeutic jurisprudence has developed, more social workers are becoming involved in therapeutic law projects. In specialized courts dealing with issues such as domestic violence, child welfare, and drugs, court personnel have developed interdisciplinary models that minimize the negative effects of traditional legal systems and integrate social work and other professional knowledge into the legal services and court processes. Therapeutic jurisprudence asks policy makers, judges, lawyers, and other legal actors to examine and evaluate all the ways that the law affects individuals, families, and communities in order to improve legal outcomes (Wexler and Winick 1996).

An investigation of therapeutic outcomes does not mean that therapeutic concerns override due process, civil liberties, or civil rights (Perlin 1996). The therapeutic jurisprudence perspective merely serves to create a venue for individuals to engage in interprofessional dialogue, outcome research, and legal reform. Critics have suggested that therapeutic jurisprudence offers no new insights into the law (Sales and Shuman 1996). But therapeutic jurisprudence is only a perspective and therefore relies on existing jurisprudential methods to achieve its goals. The unique contribution of the therapeutic jurisprudence perspective is its indeterminacy (Madden and Wayne, in press). The perspective seeks recognition of the normative values of legal decisions without determining which values should take priority. Therapeutic jurisprudence crosses professional boundaries and creates a climate that supports interprofessional collaboration and creative problem solving. It supports the application of the knowledge, skills, and techniques of many professions in order to achieve a more therapeutic experience for those involved in the legal system.

PREVENTIVE LAW

Some scholars and practitioners have begun to explore issues in how the law is practiced. Are there ways to anticipate client situations that could lead to adversarial litigation and for which the lawyer and client could proactively plan preventive action (Patry et al. 1998)? Corporate attorneys historically have used preventive law methods to keep their companies out of expensive litigation. When used in legal practice with vulnerable clients, preventive law strategies advance the goals of therapeutic jurisprudence (Stolle and Wexler 1997). Preventive law is a style of practicing law that increases opportunities for legal decision making without recourse to the courts (Hafemeister 1999). Through careful client interviewing and counseling, sound planning, and the foresight to draft agreements to avoid potential future conflicts, lawyers practicing preventive law can reduce antitherapeutic consequences (Patry et al. 1998).

The strategies used in a preventive law approach are common to good lawyers and social workers. The techniques include careful client counseling, a focus on empowering clients, and a thorough assessment of clients and their environments. Preventive approaches focus on anticipating legal needs rather than responding to legal crises. A client who is HIV positive and has a young child may need a guardianship document that becomes effective if the child requires a guardian's care because of the client's illness. Without a preventive law orientation the attorney might not become involved until a dispute arises among relatives, each seeking custody of the child while the client is incapacitated and unable to voice her wishes. Like the goals of therapeutic jurisprudence, preventive law techniques seek to improve the experiences of people involved in a legal matter by maximizing client self-determination and minimizing antitherapeutic outcomes.

The legal system operates with important structures, procedures, and policies to ensure the protection of individual rights and an ordered process for the resolution of conflicts. Many recent reform movements acknowledge the positive aspects of being a lawyer but question the reliance on the competitive, adversarial system in which one side must lose for the other side to win. Instead, these reform movements are focusing on changing the socialization that occurs in legal education and are advocating for more humane, collaborative legal practice. The phrase "ethic of care" increasingly appears in the professional literature concerning the practice of law. Although this might surprise some, it reflects a growing movement in the legal community to humanize and personalize the practice of law by building relationships and fashioning the best outcomes for people and their communities.

3.

THE DEVELOPMENT OF THE LAW

Again, there is no liberty if the judiciary power be not separated
from the legislative and executive. —Montesquieu

JUDICIAL, LEGISLATIVE, AND
ADMINISTRATIVE PROCESSES

The basic design of the U.S. legal system is distinguished by the careful placement of checks and balances on the exercise of government power. Any examination of the authority and scope of duty of the branches of government must
begin with an understanding of the concept generally referred to as the separation of powers. In the United States this concept has important historical antecedents and reflects significant values. The three branches of government are
the legislature, executive, and judiciary. In the sections that follow, I will explore the structures and processes for developing laws on the federal, state, and
local levels.

People who are not lawyers—and sometimes even those who are—find it
difficult to understand whether a legal issue involves state or federal law. How
does one determine what court hears a case? How does the law remain stable
enough to provide guidance and security for citizens while remaining flexible
enough to meet the changing needs of society? How does a social worker come
to understand the legal principles that influence professional practice and the
mechanisms for changing the law? The law is a complex phenomenon, but understanding and appreciating the underlying processes and structures is a good
way to become comfortable with legal issues.

Most newcomers to the study of law suppose that the law has a level of objectivity. Given a set of facts, a lawyer should be able to identify the legal rules
that apply and represent a client effectively by advising the client what the law
says about the situation or by making these arguments in court. The truth is

that the law in some areas does approach objectivity, laying out the "rule of law" in a way that provides determinate answers to some legal questions. In other areas, however, the law is silent about the rights or duties of people in many life circumstances (Greenawalt 1992). Unfortunately, the law provides no clear guidance for social workers in a number of practice situations.

Take, for example, the question of whether the protections in a privileged communication statute, which allow a client to keep private all information related to treatment with a clinical social worker, cover the other members of a therapy group run by the social worker. Could a group member be required to testify about the statements of another group member who was involved in a legal case? It would be comforting to be able to inform prospective group members that the statute protects all personal information and communications discussed within the group. But most states' privileged communication statutes are silent on this issue. The case law analyzing the statutes has reached different conclusions. The social worker is left with an unclear answer to a legal question directly affecting practice.

Perhaps the law should remain indeterminate in such situations in order to provide justice in each individual case. I would argue that, more likely, the legal rule has not yet been developed because of the newness of the situation (the recent passage of statutes allowing privileged communication for social workers and other psychotherapists, and the scarcity of cases deciding whether group communications are privileged) and the inability of legislation to address effectively all situations related to a new law. In this case social workers could lobby the legislature to amend the law, provide expert testimony in a court case, or work through their professional organizations such as the National Association of Social Workers (NASW) to prepare a legal brief in case an appellate court decides to review the issue. Using these strategies, social workers can advance the law related to practice rather than just react to adverse laws or judicial decisions.

THE PRIMACY OF CONSTITUTIONAL LAW

A constitution articulates the powers of a government and enumerates the organization, functions, authority, and fundamental principles that regulate the relations between a government and its citizens. A constitution prescribes the plan and method for administering the public affairs of the nation or state (*Black's* 1983). The U.S. Constitution, as interpreted by the Supreme Court, is the "supreme Law of the Land" (Article VI). Each state has its own constitution, setting forth the structures of its government and the rights of its citizens, but the U.S. Constitution remains the ultimate legal authority.

One of the most important elements of the Constitution is its delineation in the Bill of Rights (Amendments 1 through 10) of the limits on government powers and the rights of individual citizens. The balance between government power and individual rights is at the heart of public debates about controversial topics such as school desegregation, abortion, flag burning, and school prayer. The government may limit the liberties accorded to each individual only to the degree necessary to ensure that every other individual has the same right to enjoy these freedoms. In addition, the Bill of Rights limits government power in order to avoid unjust interference with individual liberties, guaranteeing freedom from unreasonable searches, freedom of association, and freedom of speech, among others. The amendments require procedural devices to ensure proper government behavior. For example, due process (timely notice and a hearing before a government can take an action against an individual), and probable cause hearings (held to determine whether a court can authorize government search-and-seizure actions) protect individual rights. I will discuss these and other constitutional protections in greater detail in subsequent chapters, but here I want to stress the importance of appreciating the enormous influence of the Constitution on the everyday life experiences of each citizen.

A less familiar but no less important element of the Constitution is the manner in which it defines the relative power of the national and state governments and sets out the role of each of the three branches of the federal government, allocating federal power among the branches. The balance of power created by the tripartite system of government is designed to ensure that no individual or institution assumes too much power. Congress may pass a law, or the president may direct an administrator to adopt a policy, but if these actions are in conflict with the Constitution, they will be invalidated if challenged in court.

The Constitution also defines the powers and rights that the individual states retain. The Tenth Amendment establishes that the power of the federal government is not absolute. The state retains any power that the Constitution does not specifically delegate to the federal government. However, the federal judiciary may review state law and the actions of state officials for constitutionality. Although the Constitution does not explicitly give the courts the power to determine what is constitutional, the Supreme Court, ruling in *McCulloch v. Maryland* (1819), determined that state actions are invalid if they interfere with the Constitution and the laws and treaties passed pursuant to it.

The Supreme Court's authority to have the final say in interpreting the Constitution guides the development of federal law. This authority was clarified in a case from 1803 that involved a classic political struggle, not unlike that which surrounded the 2000 presidential election. Just before leaving his term of office as president, John Adams sought to enhance his political legacy by naming a number of new judges who shared his Federalist views. On taking office, Thomas Jefferson, a Democratic-Republican, refused to honor those appointments where the actual judicial commissions had not yet been delivered. Several of the judges affected filed suit, asking the Supreme Court to use the power granted to it by an act of Congress (the Judiciary Act of 1801) to order the president to recognize their appointments (*Marbury v. Madison* [1803]).

The details of the case are less important than the outcome. Justice John Marshall, in perhaps the most significant Supreme Court decision in history, concluded that the Judiciary Act itself was unconstitutional because it sought to give an area of jurisdiction to the Supreme Court not found in the Constitution. Marshall thus refused to issue the order sought by the judges. He concluded that if the Supreme Court identifies a conflict between a statute and a constitutional provision, the Court has the authority and the duty to declare the statute unconstitutional and to invalidate it. The decision affirmed the principle of judicial review. That is, determining constitutional questions is the role of the judiciary, not Congress.

The principle of judicial review is essential to understanding the development of the law in a number of ways. First, because federal judges are appointed for life, they theoretically are able to remain above politics, whereas Congress is subject to the pressures of retaining office. This security allows for a more independent judiciary, able to listen to the views of minority or oppressed populations without worrying about the effect on an election or maintaining popularity. A judge is thus more likely to undertake a legal analysis of a statute rather than a political one. Second, although the legislature has the power to enact laws, the principle of judicial review serves as a check on overzealous use of this authority by a political body. The law evolves but retains stability through the judicial review process. Finally, well-reasoned judicial review is necessary to fine-tune broadly written statutory language in order to delineate the the law's scope and its applicability to a variety of factual situations.

The relationship among the Constitution, state constitutions, federal and state laws, administrative regulations, court decisions, and legal rules is complex, but a few key concepts illuminate the logical structure of this system. It is helpful to think about a hierarchy of authority in which law made at one level might be invalidated by the actions of a higher legal entity. Because the Constitution is the supreme law of the land, no laws, regulations, or case decisions can conflict with its principles. In the context of state law the state constitution is the supreme authority, although the rulings of a state supreme court can be appealed to the U.S. Supreme Court.

Historically, the enumerated powers specifically granted to the federal government by the Constitution have limited the authority of the federal government. The framers of the Constitution established the United States as a federalist system. Because of the American colonists' negative experiences with being governed by a distant centralized power, the framers gave the states general authority over the health and welfare of their citizens. Thus a state has rule-making authority in all areas except those limited by the Constitution, whereas the authority of the federal government authority is limited to those areas specified within the Constitution (Art. 1, sect. 8).

In some areas both the states and the federal government may have a claim to legislate. The concept of preemption holds that where the federal government has established a rule on a matter that involves national interests, a state law conflicting with it is preempted (*Black's* 1983). State law is also preempted in those areas where Congress has explicitly or implicitly prohibited state regulation (Vandevelde 1998). The need to establish consistency of laws to support interstate commerce has been the primary focus of the preemption doctrine.

For example, the federal statute known as ERISA (Employee Retirement Income Security Act of 1974) protects the interests of workers who participate in private employment benefit plans. The national interest is in maintaining one standard set of rules for employee benefits so that companies with workers in multiple states would not have to follow different rules in each location. The argument that ERISA preempts state action has defeated some state attempts to regulate managed care. Because of the broad reach of this statute, courts have dismissed many attempts to sue because of negligent managed-care decisions. Political support for maintaining the ERISA preemption has waned, so Congress is likely to rewrite the ERISA statute to allow legal challenges of medical decisions made by managed-care companies.

Federal authority has expanded and extended beyond the specific roles listed in the Constitution. The Supreme Court established the doctrine of implied powers in *McCulloch v. Maryland* (1819). The doctrine allows Congress to make laws that are necessary and proper for carrying out the enumerated functions. Before the Civil War most congressional activity involved the regulation of interstate commerce. But paralleling the move toward war was the transformation of the United States from an agrarian to an industrialized society, and the latter required the federal government to exercise its full range of powers. For example, the development of canals, toll roads, and railroads produced a dramatic increase in interstate commerce and transportation, along with the rise of national companies. This development prompted Congress to enact new laws regulating business transactions. The new laws established federal enforcement agencies (such as the Securities and Exchange Commission), which assumed powers formerly retained by the states (Ehrlich 2000).

Initially, federal criminal law was directed at crimes against the United States such as treason. Later Congress addressed the regulation of commercial activities. In recent years Congress has passed a number of federal criminal statutes in response to high-profile problems such as school shootings, drug dealing, and organized crime (Ehrlich 2000). Federal police organizations such as the Federal Bureau of Investigation; the Bureau of Alcohol, Tobacco, and Firearms; and the Drug Enforcement Administration have grown proportionally with the development of these laws. The trend has raised concerns about a growing concentration of power in the federal government.

Growing federal power and an expanded scope of federal involvement in people's lives characterized the period from the New Deal through the early 1990s because of a broad notion of what constituted a national issue. In response to an increasingly conservative political mood in the country since the 1980s, the legislative and executive branches have supported a process of devolution, returning to the states many powers and responsibilities that the federal government had gradually assumed (Schneider and Lester 2001). The primary limitation on the exercise of federal power is that it not conflict with any constitutional prohibitions (Tribe 1988). Recently, it appears that the Supreme Court is joining the movement to limit the scope of federal authority, especially in its recent rulings interpreting the commerce clause (Lens 2001).

The commerce clause gives the federal government the power to regulate interstate commerce. During the twentieth century, the Supreme Court used the commerce clause to decide a number of cases related to civil rights. The rationale for these cases was that discrimination affected interstate commerce. Recently, the Court struck down the Violence Against Women Act (*United States v. Morrison* [2000]) and the Guns-Free School Zones Act (*United States v. Lopez* [1995]), reasoning that these areas are not closely connected to commerce or economic activity and are areas traditionally regulated by the states. The Supreme Court concluded that the federal government cannot regulate these types of activities under the commerce clause. As a result, the federal statutes related to civil rights and social welfare are in jeopardy of being overturned, and Congress seems unlikely to pursue new laws in these areas, preferring to leave these matters to the states (Lens 2001).

The doctrine of legislative supremacy requires courts to apply the law as written in the statutes, even if it conflicts with common law (case law). Occasionally, courts interpret statutes to achieve a desired result in a case or in a manner that frustrates the legislative purpose. The federal and state legislatures have the authority to enact a law to overturn a court's decision (Vandevelde 1998). Since the early 1900s legislatures have become far more active in enacting measures that cover many specific areas of the law. Where once a search of applicable law began with looking at cases (the common law), today most attorneys begin with a review of relevant statutes (Price, Bitner, and Bysiewicz 1979).

Legislation enacted by Congress or by the legislature of a state may directly address societal needs and problems. Often a legislature will develop broad goals or delegate rule-making authority to the executive branch (i.e., the president or governor and their respective administrations). In these cases the relevant administrative agencies with expertise in the subject receive limited authority to develop regulations to implement the legislative goals. This type of rule making is called subordinate legislation in that the enabling statute prevails if the stated goals of the legislation and the eventual regulations developed by the administrative agency are in conflict (Price, Bitner, and Bysiewicz 1979). Also, the delegation of rule-making authority is proper only if the legislature provided the administrative agency with sufficient standards (LaFave 1988).

LAWMAKING: FROM SOCIETAL NEEDS TO RULES TO PRINCIPLES

The law is the witness and external deposit of our moral life.

—Oliver Wendell Holmes

Laws can be characterized in terms of whether they impose a duty, confer a right, or grant a power (Saltzman and Proch 1990). Laws are society's tools for defining what behavior is impermissible and what happens to those whose conduct violates a rule. Laws also define the rules for managing the legal system, that is, for managing the way in which the government enforces the laws through its police and judicial systems to protect individual rights. Dernbach and Singleton

(1981) describe the importance of legal rules as a means of avoiding or resolving disputes peaceably and predictably, of promoting socially desirable goals and defining relationships among people, and of increasing security and confidence in daily interactions by enforcing legally protected rights (2–3). When it works effectively, the law establishes common expectations of the rules of relationships among people and between the government and the people.

Understanding the process of lawmaking is important. At various points a social worker might play a role in creating or modifying a law for the benefit of clients or the profession. The following example concerns a relatively new New Jersey law enacted to respond to the problem of domestic violence, especially harassing and violent actions directed at women.

Javonda, a registered nurse, had known Keith for many years. Keith and Javonda were never romantically involved. Nonetheless, Keith would repeatedly stand at the gate of the hospital's employee parking lot when Javonda arrived for work at 7:15 A.M. and when she left work at about 4 P.M. During these times he would stand and watch Javonda. His actions so frightened her that she reported his conduct to the police. The incidents continued and on a couple of occasions Keith attempted to interact with Javonda. One day he approached the passenger side of Javonda's vehicle. He got within five feet of her car, which frightened Javonda so much that she drove through a red light. Later that day Keith again was standing and watching outside the hospital when Javonda left work. She reported Keith's conduct to the police, who arrested him and charged him with stalking. At the trial Keith testified and denied that he intended to harass, frighten, or annoy Javonda. He explained that he frequented the neighborhood to visit friends. He also stated that he was in the area on several occasions because he had legitimate business at the hospital.

Keith was convicted on the charge of stalking. He appealed, contending that the stalking statute (N.J. Stat. Ann. 2C:12–10 [West 2001]) violates both the federal and New Jersey Constitutions because it is vague and overly broad. In other words, he argued that the law, as written, was not specific enough in the conduct that it described to give a person fair notice that the behavior was an illegal activity. Further, the argument suggests that because the language of the law was so broadly written, it might prohibit some activities that the U.S. Constitution protects. Keith contended that his actions were protected under the First Amendment as "expressive activities" (*State v. Saunders* [1997]).

When an area of the law is new, those charged, convicted, or otherwise held liable under its terms often challenge the law. In *Saunders* the defendant argued that the new law violated constitutional principles. His legal challenge went to the heart of the purpose of stalking laws: to intervene in repetitive harassing or threatening behavior before the victim has actually been physically attacked. The New Jersey Superior Court, in response to an appeal, ruled that so long as the harassment statute required a specific intent to harass the victim, it was constitutional as a reasonable restriction on the manner in which speech is expressed, regardless of its content. The appellate court found that the jury's determination that Keith intended his actions to harm was justified (i.e., he must have known that his actions would reasonably cause Javonda to fear that she was at risk). The court's decision clarified the rule in stalking cases: Freedom of speech does not encompass a right to abuse or annoy another person intentionally.

Examining the history of the laws against stalking is instructive. Flynn has characterized stalking as behavior exceeding harassment but not yet advanced to assault or other, more serious crimes that involve overt threats or physical contact (1993). Stalking laws developed as part of a response to the societal goal of eliminating harassment and other forms of violence, especially as directed toward women. Historically, police had few answers to complaints of stalking. Because no statutes specifically targeted stalking behaviors, police argued that they were powerless to make an arrest unless the stalker carried out a violent act. Beyond civil restraining orders (which historically lacked any serious sanctions), a victim of such behavior had no legal recourse.

As part of the changing social conditions involving gender, especially the movement of more women into the paid workforce, various social policies supporting equality emerged. One fundamental legal principle arising from this advancement of equality is the right to be free from harassment and unwelcome sexual advances. In addition to the stalking laws, state and federal legislatures passed a variety of legislation to support the same social value, such as the gender discrimination provisions of Title VII of the Civil Rights Act of 1964 and the right to sue for sexual harassment in the workplace (Flynn 1993). One can argue about whether the collective rules have established the legal principle or whether societal recognition of the principle was the impetus for developing these legal rules. Regardless, the result is the same: a changing legal landscape that provides increased protection for women's equal status in economic and social settings.

Social workers can have an influence on the development of laws such as the stalking statutes. Several years ago, at a public hearing of the Judiciary Committee of the Connecticut General Assembly, I sat waiting to testify on a child welfare bill. The Judiciary Committee was concluding testimony on a proposal to establish an antistalking law. The comments of several influential legislators made it clear that they had grave concerns about a statute that would criminally sanction one person for being near another person or perhaps even for telephoning a former lover after an argument. A young woman approached the desk to testify about her experiences of being stalked by a former boyfriend. The usually intrepid legislators were captivated and moved by her story; as she spoke, other committee members emerged from their offices to listen to what she was saying. The committee approved bill, and it was subsequently signed into law. Social workers can empower clients to tell their stories to lawmakers, thereby attaching a real face to the issue. Social workers may also be involved in progressive legal reforms by becoming directly involved in developing case law. As I discuss the common law process later in the chapter, consider where in the process social work advocacy (e.g., enabling clients to gain access to legal representation, providing direct testimony about a client's situation, or serving as an expert witness) could influence the development of more just and effective laws.

COMPARING CRIMINAL AND CIVIL LAW PROCEDURES

A criminal case is an action taken to identify and punish a defendant for an act that violates a criminal statute. A criminal act is a wrong committed against a victim, but the law also considers it to be an action that affects society. As a result, the state or federal government prosecutes criminal acts at public expense, in the name of the people (Barker and Branson 2000). Because a criminal prosecution is an action by the government that is directed at an individual, constitutional protections for individual rights are of utmost importance. The concern about the arbitrary power of political authority was foremost in the minds of the framers of the Constitution, resulting in a system of criminal procedure that places heavy burdens on the government to prove the guilt of an individual before restricting that person's liberty.

In contrast, a civil case is a noncriminal lawsuit. It is a means of settling disputes between two parties. Civil cases involve many types of disputes, including family matters, contracts, property, and torts. A tort is an action (or sometimes an omission) recognized by the law that causes harm to another party. It includes negligent actions, for example, in accidents or malpractice claims. A tort may also be an intentional act such as slander, libel, or assault. In some circumstances a criminal trial may be followed by a civil trial: the former to prosecute an alleged crime and the latter for the injured party to seek damages. Perhaps the most notorious example of this in recent years is the O. J. Simpson saga; he was cleared of criminal charges but was found to be liable for damages in civil court.

The Sixth Amendment to the Constitution provides that in all criminal prosecutions, the accused shall enjoy the right to have the assistance of counsel for her or his defense. Criminal procedure guarantees the appointment of an attorney if an accused person cannot afford one; requires a *Miranda* warning at the time of arrest, informing the individual of her or his rights; circumscribes the permissible behaviors of the police; and generally operates to limit the arbitrary use of power by the government. Being a party to a civil suit does not guarantee representation by an attorney, except for those cases where state law provides for legal aid, such as lawyers appointed for children or other groups with limited ability to voice their point of view in court.

The rules that define criminal behavior must be specific and detailed in order to give notice to the public of what behavior is against the law. The prosecution must prove the defendant's guilt beyond a reasonable doubt. Most crimes have two basic elements, an act and a mental state. In order to obtain a finding of guilt the state must prove every element of the crime. This requirement has significant influence on legislative decisions about how to define and classify a crime (LaFave 1988). For example, if a crime requires intent as an element, the prosecution has the burden of proving this element of the crime. Some areas of civil law are equally specific in detailing the elements of a cause of action (such as commercial transactions, child welfare laws), but the legislature intentionally leaves vague the details of many categories of civil law so that it can be flexible as new factual situations and societal conditions emerge.

The legal term *burden of proof* has two elements. The party given responsibility for proving an element of a case is said to have the "burden of production," that is, producing evidence that supports the point. In a criminal case the burden of production is generally on the prosecutor, although some exceptions exist, such as when a defendant asserts self-defense. In these cases the state has the initial burden of producing evidence that the incident occurred, at which point the burden shifts to the defendant. The shifting burden, also applicable in some civil cases, can be thought of as a "yes but" defense, acknowledging that the events occurred but producing evidence to show the defendant's acts were justified or excusable.

The second element of burden of proof is the level of certainty that the proof must provide. In criminal cases the burden is for the state to prove a case beyond a reasonable doubt. This level ensures that the government has overwhelming justification for curtailing a person's liberty. In a civil case the plaintiff usually must prove a case by a preponderance of the evidence. That means that, when weighed against the evidence of the opposing party, the plaintiff's evidence is more convincing and thus more likely to represent the truth. In some cases policy reasons have caused the legislature to require a higher burden of proof, a standard of "clear and convincing" evidence. Usually, the legislature uses this standard when the risk of harm to a class of defendants is significant if the case is decided against them (e.g., denaturalization hearings, fraud allegations).

I will discuss the criminal process in more detail in chapter 6 and the civil law process in chapters 7 and 8. However, understanding the different elements of criminal and civil procedure as they relate to the purpose of the courts is important. In the criminal context the priority is to protect individual rights from unjustified actions of the government. In the civil context the priority is to fairly balance the rights of the parties to have their day in court while protecting the interests of the party against whom the case has been filed. In both situations the court has an interest in structures that can resolve issues reliably and efficiently.

THE STRUCTURE OF THE COURT SYSTEM

State and federal courts are structured in similar ways, resulting in a logical system for managing various types of litigation. Sometimes social workers and other professionals react too strongly to the decision in a single court case (Madden 1998). The case may stand out as a significant legal ruling, but it may not reflect an accurate legal rule. It is important to understand the relationship between the role of the particular court that decided the case and the degree to which the decision has the power to influence subsequent cases. The identity of the court tells a great deal about whether the ruling is a final one and whether it has anything to say directly about the law in a particular jurisdiction.

STATE COURT SYSTEMS

The names of the courts in each state vary, but the basic three-level design is the common model for states. States generally have two levels of trial court. The first, historically called courts of limited jurisdiction, hear civil cases in which the damage amount is small, and they hear simple criminal cases, usually involving misdemeanors. Sometimes these courts are referred to as justice courts because originally a justice of the peace presided over them. In cities these courts are called municipal courts, and the judges may be referred to as magistrates (Louisell, Hazard, and Tait 1983).

The second type of state trial court is a court of general jurisdiction. The states have various names for these courts such as Superior Court (California), Supreme Court (New York), and circuit, county, and district courts. One judge usually hears trials in these courts. Increasingly, the states are establishing specialized trial courts to handle cases related to particular issues or populations, such as family courts, juvenile courts, and recently, in recognition of the unique knowledge base required by complex social issues, the development of drug courts, domestic violence courts, and housing courts, among others.

A plaintiff or a defendant may appeal the decision of a trial court. The appellate court reviews issues of law, such as whether the trial court properly applied a statute or correctly interpreted the common law, whether the trial judge made any errors in allowing consideration of evidence, and whether the jury was properly instructed as to the law. Again, the names and exact structure of the appellate division vary by state, but three-judge panels often hear the appeal.

The highest level of appellate court in each state is the state supreme court. Usually composed of seven justices, these courts act much like the U.S. Supreme Court in that they decide only those cases that they select. A lawyer can request a hearing before the state supreme court by filing a request called a writ of certiorari. If the ruling of an intermediate appellate court departs from precedent, raises a new issue (an issue of first impression), or has significance for the advancement of state law, the state supreme court may choose to hear the case. The decisions of a state supreme court can be appealed to the U.S. Supreme Court in some circumstances. If the issue decided in the case addresses an issue of federal law or if the ruling has constitutional implications, the Supreme Court may accept the case for review, but its review is limited to the federal question.

THE FEDERAL COURT SYSTEM

The initial question to be considered in a federal court is whether the court has jurisdiction to hear the case. Recall that state statutes control most areas of the law; thus state courts should hear cases on these issues. Sometimes the federal courts are the appropriate venue for a case. These circumstances fall into two general categories. First, if the conflict at the heart of the case involves citizens or corporations residing in different states and the amount in conflict is more than $75,000, the federal courts can hear the case based on diversity jurisdiction (28 U.S.C. 1332). Also, if a case raises a federal question involving the Constitution or a federal statute or regulation, or if the case involves federal agencies, the case may be heard in the federal trial court (28 U.S.C. 1331).

Lawyers preparing a case often examine the relative merits of bringing a case in a state versus a federal court. At times, particular decisions or rules might favor one jurisdiction over another; therefore, the preliminary battle over where to have the trial could determine the outcome. When discussing the need for an advocacy suit such as a class action on behalf of an underserved group, social workers need to be aware that an attorney may seek to frame the legal issues in a way that makes it possible to choose the court that will hear the case. The recent trend has been to reduce the scope of issues that may be brought on the federal level (Lens 2001).

The federal trial courts are called district courts. Each district comprises a section of the country, and its judges sit as trial judges hearing cases. The federal court must apply the substantive law of the relevant state, unless it is superseded by a federal law (*Erie Railroad v. Tompkins* [1938]). Appeals of trial court rulings go to one of the thirteen circuits of the U.S. Court of Appeals, twelve for various areas of the country and one for the Federal Circuit. Here, judges usually sit in three-judge panels to hear appeals, although occasionally, the circuit court justices may sit en banc (all the justices of the court compose the panel) to hear an appeal.

The U.S. Supreme Court has original jurisdiction over cases involving conflicts between states. In addition to taking limited appeals from the state supreme courts that involve a federal question, the Supreme Court has authority to accept an appeal (called a writ of certiorari) from an appellate court decision. The Court neither acts upon nor rejects most requests for certiorari. The Court selects its docket by using a screening system that requires that four of the seven justices vote to hear a case. Sometimes the justices will search for a case that addresses an important issue that has been in conflict in the various circuit courts. The appellate courts may ask the Supreme Court directly to accept this type of appeal in order to clarify the rule of law on the question in conflict. Other times, the Supreme Court selects a case because at least four justices are prepared to use the case to make new law, to clarify a point of law, or to affirm an important principle.

The Supreme Court's ruling in the social work privilege case, *Jaffe v. Redmond* (1996), provides a good example of a case in which an appeal to the highest court was necessary. In *Jaffe* a police officer, Mary Lu Redmond, killed a suspect and subsequently sought the assistance of a licensed social worker. The family of the suspect sued Redmond and sought the social worker's records to use in cross-examining the officer. The attorneys were seeking evidence that she had admitted to things in counseling that would contradict her official version of what happened.

The trial court rejected Redmond's argument that psychotherapist-client privilege protected these communications and ordered the disclosure. When Redmond and the social worker both refused to divulge any details, the judge instructed the jury to presume that the contents of the notes would have been unfavorable to Redmond. The jury found for the plaintiff and ordered Redmond to pay significant damages to the man's estate.

Redmond appealed this decision to the U.S. Court of Appeals, which ruled that the trial court should have upheld the privilege. The appellate court reversed the decision of the trial court and ordered a new trial in compliance with its ruling on privilege. In the past various federal appellate courts had ruled differently on the recognition of a psychotherapist-client privilege under federal law. Therefore, the Supreme Court accepted the appeal. Also, some courts had used a balancing test, weighing the original promise of confidentiality against the court's need for the disclosure of all available, probative evidence in a trial. The Supreme Court rejected this approach as an evisceration of the effectiveness of the privilege and little better than no privilege at all. In order to support the important social benefits that come from people seeking the help of psychotherapists, the Court determined that confidential communications between a licensed psychotherapist and a client are protected from compelled disclosure in federal courts.

The Court acknowledged the need for exceptions to the general rule when only the disclosure by a therapist can avert a threat of serious harm. However, in a classic legal strategy the Court did not specify the scope of this exception. The Court announced only a broad rule, which allows future decisions of the lower appellate courts to develop the details regarding when the exception applies. When the law develops in response to accumulated cases that stretch the reach of a legal rule, the process is called the common law. This concept is critical to understanding the U.S. legal system and the way that lawyers must think about cases.

RULES AND CASES: COMMON LAW DEVELOPMENT

One of the great legal minds of the twentieth century, Benjamin Cardozo, reflected on the slow pace of legal development that occurs in the common law process. "The work of deciding cases goes on every day in hundreds of courts throughout the land. Any judge, one might suppose, would find it easy to describe the process which he had followed a thousand times and more. Nothing could be further from the truth" (1921:9). Cardozo's words give insight into an important truth in U.S. law: Every case involves unique personal stories and experiences. Whether the case is a divorce, bankruptcy, malpractice action, criminal charge, or child protection hearing, individuals' lives are affected by their interactions with the legal system. In trying to come to the right decision, judges are supposed to follow existing law, but they also have an obligation to consider the interests of justice, changing societal or technological conditions, and basic notions of fairness. This dynamic, repeated in courthouses every day, is what pushes the law forward incrementally and results in the uneven development of the common law.

Important legal concepts form the foundation of the common law. Its essence is judicial reliance on history and recognition of trends. The concept of precedence implies that judges should follow previous decisions of courts in cases that raise similar questions (Dernbach and Singleton 1981). Adherence to the concept of precedence increases stability and predictability in the law. Public confidence in the legitimacy of the legal system rests on the idea that court decisions have a level of objectivity and consistency. If judges were allowed to decide cases freely, without reference to past decisions, citizens would face more difficulty in knowing what the law allows, and lawyers would not be able to advise clients concerning their potential liability.

The concept of legal precedent is primarily a search for authority (Price, Bitner, and Bysiewicz 1979). Although the jury decision or trial court ruling might have influence on a court, nothing requires a judge to follow that decision. The concept of stare decisis (to stand by things that have been settled) theoretically compels a court to follow its own decisions and the decisions of higher courts within the same jurisdiction. In practice, however, judges may decide a case on an alternative legal basis or may interpret the facts of a case to avoid conflicting with a precedent. The arguments of the attorneys involved in a case reflect this process. They can present a case highlighting certain facts or arguing the applicability of controlling precedents that would require a case to be decided in their client's favor.

Applying the concept of precedence is a complicated task. The general purpose of precedence is for courts to be consistent in applying legal rules to similar factual situations. But which court decisions are binding on a judge? We must begin by recalling the structure of the court systems described earlier in this chapter. The hierarchical structure of the judiciary determines the significance of a previous decision. A verdict by a jury may be suggestive to a trial court hearing another case with similar issues. However, a jury is making a decision based on facts, so unless that ruling is appealed and a higher court rules on a point of law, the jury's decision has established no legal rule and created no precedent.

Consider, for example, a case where a jury returns a verdict in favor of the plaintiff in a malpractice suit against a social worker. The suit involved the social worker's failure to recommend a psychiatric examination of a depressed client who later committed suicide. This case might influence the attorneys in a subsequent case with identical facts to seek a settlement because it may demonstrate a probable outcome in the present case. Also, if the lawyer for the social worker sought to have the case dismissed, arguing that the facts did not support a finding of professional negligence, the judge in the second case might be influenced by the jury's verdict and allow the second case to go to trial.

When the California Supreme Court ruled in *Tarasoff* that a mental health clinician has a duty to warn a person of a potential threat, the decision was binding precedent only on California cases. However, when a prominent state supreme court decides a high-profile case, the decision can influence the courts of other jurisdictions, as *Tarasoff* has demonstrated. In searching for cases, lawyers construct a hierarchy of results, ascribing highest importance to cases from the appellate or supreme court of the jurisdiction where the case is being heard, whereas the cases from other jurisdictions and lower courts carry less authority and persuasiveness.

In the case of the social worker whose client committed suicide, consider the implications if the social worker's appeal was based on these circumstances: the social worker worked for the state child welfare agency, and the client was the parent of a child in state custody. The appeal, citing cases from the federal courts and from other states, argues that trial judge should have dismissed the case based on the doctrine of sovereign immunity (making public employees and agencies exempt from being sued). The appellate court agrees that the judge should have applied the law of sovereign immunity, finding that state social workers, operating in the scope of their professional roles, cannot be sued for malpractice, and reverses the decision. The parents then appeal to the state supreme court, which reviews the question in depth and upholds the appellate court. The highest court's ruling on the law of sovereign immunity defines the legal rule for trial and appellate courts in this jurisdiction and becomes binding precedent for any subsequent case on this question.

The common law is a fluid, developing system. It seems inconsistent to suggest that the issue of suing a state social worker for malpractice is decided for all time after this case. The common law process enables the modification of legal rules by using several legal arguments. Distinguishing previous cases from the facts of the current case can provide the court with sufficient flexibility to avoid following a binding precedent. The legal argument focuses on reconciling the contrary precedent with the desired outcome in the case (Vandevelde 1998).

Consider the facts of a different malpractice case. The suicide was a child who was under the care and custody of the state. The state social worker had responsibility to see the child at least once each month. On one visit the child was depressed and withdrawn. The social worker failed to visit the child for two months because of vacation and the demands of a high caseload. Soon after, the child committed suicide. A lawyer arguing this case might highlight the involvement of a minor, not an adult, as in the first case. The lawyer might argue that this creates a different and greater duty on the part of the social worker. A court would have discretion to carve out a new rule, not overruling the previously announced rule but extending the common law to include the newly defined duty.

Stare decisis creates a strong presumption against overturning legal rules (Vandevelde 1998). To the extent that the legal rule has been applied consistently and clarified by specific cases, the force of the precedent is strong and a court is likely to follow it. When a legal rule has been announced in a previous case, a judge can determine that the ruling was dictum rather than the holding of a case. As discussed previously, dictum is part of a judge's opinion but is not the technical legal holding. It may be influential but need not be followed by later decisions. When a legal rule is based on a policy rationale that has become outdated, a court has the discretion to directly overrule a precedent, creating a new legal rule.

In summary, the common law is a constantly evolving system that allows legal professionals to interpret what the law requires and to predict how a court might decide a case. Are there clear legal rules that would be applied to decide a case, or do the facts implicate an alternative legal rule? Is the precedent strongly supported by current social conditions, or can it be argued that a new legal rule is necessary? It is up to a judge to decide how a legal rule applies to the facts of a situation. It is here that many cases make a deductive form of legal thinking unfulfilling. A judge must use discretion to apply the law. The common law process enables a judge to decide cases by balancing the stability and predictability that come from clear legal rules with the flexibility to decide individual cases through an application of reason and justice.

4.

THE PRACTICE OF LAW

It is the trade of lawyers to question everything, yield nothing,
and to talk by the hour. —Thomas Jefferson

THE ADVOCACY SYSTEM AND THE ROLES
OF LEGAL PROFESSIONALS

Throughout history the fashion has been to stereotype lawyers with negative characterizations peppered with such adjectives as *greedy, sleazy, amoral,* and *unyielding.* Yet when faced with a life situation in which legal representation is required, every person wants an attorney who will do everything possible to protect the client's personal rights and to achieve positive outcomes. The truth is that most lawyers take pride in assuming the advocacy role and take care to practice with rigorous adherence to ethical standards. As in social work, a set of professional values guides a lawyer's actions. Social workers need to develop an appreciation of the influence of these values on the roles and behaviors that lawyers assume in practice.

Lawyers are expected to prioritize the needs of their clients, representing them with zeal and a commitment to furthering their interests. Fundamental to the attorney-client relationship is maintaining honest communication and strict confidentiality. At the same time a lawyer is an officer of the court, bound to serve the law and to advance the work of justice (Kronman 1998). If these fragmented alliances sound familiar, it is because they are similar to the expectations in social work practice. The tension between providing social care to a client and having a responsibility to society for social control is familiar (Congress 1999). Lawyers struggle with the same types of practice dilemmas as social workers in trying to balance advocacy and protection to always act in the client's best interest.

If we distill the practice of law, we can identify three prominent features:

1. Because of the power and authority allocated to the individuals and institutions comprising the legal system, legal professionals are involved with the creation, application, and modification of rules that govern societal relationships (Sunstein 1996).
2. The common experience of all attorneys includes playing a role in controversies or potential controversies between people or between a person and the state.
3. Most legal settings use an adversarial process to resolve disputes.

When we examine these three factors together, it is apparent how some lawyers cross the line of appropriate professional standards. Lawyers are accorded prestige because of their highly specialized role in lawmaking, law enforcement, and protection of individual rights. The resulting power and authority can become intoxicating and effective weapons in the midst of controversy. However, expectations of professional conduct mitigate the indiscriminate use of power and authority.

A comparison to the practice of social work is useful to illustrate how legal professionals are drawn into questionable behavior. Social workers who find themselves in legal trouble often have made poor choices based on good motives (Madden 1998). For example, a social worker working with a divorcing couple feels strongly that the husband is more capable of providing a safe, nurturing environment for the children because of the wife's psychiatric condition. At the request of the husband the social worker writes a letter to the court expressing concerns about the wife's competence, without securing permission from the wife to release confidential information. The social worker may have acted with good intentions to protect the children from being placed in the care of an impaired parent, but she failed to follow the legal requirements for securing permission to release the information.

As social workers, we can appreciate how this situation occurred, even as we recognize what was improper about the social worker's conduct. Similarly, a community organizer who uses questionable tactics to further an important goal is regarded as having pure motives, even if the fervor of his convictions caused a lack of good judgment in the selection of means. We often fail to extend the same courtesy, of giving deference to good intentions, to lawyers whose behavior or demeanor comes into question.

FIRST PRINCIPLES OF LEGAL PRACTICE

To develop a deeper understanding of the thoughts and actions of attorneys, it is important to begin with the principles most important to their practice. The first principles of legal practice are articulated in the *Model Rules of Professional Conduct* of the American Bar Association (ABA 1999, hereafter, *Model Rules*) and include

The fiduciary nature of the attorney-client relationship
The fundamental importance of attorney-client privilege and the confidentiality of a client's information
The role of the advocacy system in reaching just results
The value of preparation and competence to effective lawyering

THE FIDUCIARY NATURE OF THE LAWYER-CLIENT RELATION-SHIPS. Lawyers serve as agents for their clients. In this capacity they act on behalf of clients who have entrusted their lawyers to protect their legal rights and privileges. As agents, lawyers bear a substantial responsibility to put their clients' interests first in all interactions. In effect, we can say that the standard of care for lawyers is to act with scrupulous good faith and candor (*Black's* 1983) and to act with integrity in undertaking all the responsibilities implied in legal representation.

The fundamental components of the lawyer-client relationship are loyalty to the client (ABA 1999:rule 1.7) and respect for client autonomy (rule 1.2). These rules proscribe conflicts of interest and reinforce the rights of clients to manage most aspects of their representation. In specific areas, such as the cost and objectives of the representation, the decision to appeal a ruling, or whether to accept a settlement or plea bargain, a lawyer must seek direction from the client before acting. A lawyer retains the responsibility of selecting the technical and legal tactical issues. It is helpful to understand the relationship between an attorney and a client as a partnership. The client directs the course of the representation, and the lawyer uses professional judgment and discretion to maximize the client's interests.

An important distinction lies in the fiduciary duty of various legal officials. Judicial personnel, lawyers for administrative agencies, and law enforcement officials such as district attorneys and prosecutors owe primary allegiance to the system rather than to the individual. An attorney for an individual or a corporation is required to represent the interests of the client. For this reason a lawyer appointed by an insurance company to handle a lawsuit against a social worker has primary allegiance to the insurance company to limit the amount of any claims. At times this role might contradict the interests of the social worker, leaving the social worker vulnerable if the social worker has not obtained independent legal counsel. In any legal interaction social workers initially must try to determine who the lawyer represents in order to understand the lawyer's fiduciary responsibilities to that client.

For example, social workers frequently interact with families that need help managing legal issues for elderly people whose cognitive functioning is declining because of dementia. A lawyer representing the elderly person may not be inclined to automatically follow the wishes of family members to draw up a power of attorney that gives a relative the right to manage the financial affairs of the client. Representing the elderly client is not the same as providing a legal service to the family. The lawyer must be reasonably sure that the individual has the capacity to understand what is being signed. If not, the appropriate legal strategy is to ask the probate court to appoint a guardian to protect the interests of the client (J. Rosenberg 2000). Even when family members seem to be trying to act in the best interests of the client, the lawyer's fiduciary duty to the client directs and controls the process.

A social worker helping this family might experience the lawyer's insistence on taking this extra legal step as unduly time consuming, technical, and costly. Once social workers recognize that the basis of the lawyer's action is a professional ethical mandate, they are likely to view the lawyer's motives differently, which should help interprofessional collaboration. The social worker also may be able to assist the family to understand and accept the legal process.

ATTORNEY-CLIENT PRIVILEGE AND CLIENT CONFIDENTIALITY. Two related aspects of confidentiality in legal practice mirror the confidentiality protections in social work practice. First, every jurisdiction recognizes attorney-client privilege in evidence law. These laws protect client information by preventing lawyers from having to testify or give evidence about their clients in judicial or other legal proceedings (Morgan and Rotunda 1988). The law also shields the work product of a lawyer, such as interviews or research compiled in the course of representing a client. The need for statutory protection of attorney-client communications is obvious. Clients must be able to be forthright with their lawyers concerning all the facts in a legal situation, including ones that could incriminate them, in order for lawyers to provide effective representation.

The second level of confidentiality is a general ethical duty, broader than the statutory privilege, that prevents an attorney from revealing evidence against a client. Client confidentiality is crucial to legal practice. Information disclosed by a client to an attorney is often incriminating. Breaches of confidentiality or sharing information beyond a client's consent could have financial or legal consequences, in addition to potential damage to a client's reputation. The adherence to strict client confidentiality is a value of extraordinary importance to and a fundamental belief of a practicing attorney (Hazard 1999). Failure to maintain confidentiality is treated seriously in disciplinary cases and could result in the loss of a lawyer's license to practice (ABA 1999:rule 1.6).

As in social work practice, some exceptions exist to the general rule of confidentiality in a lawyer-client relationship. The most notable one is the crime and/or fraud exception, which denies protection to communications in furtherance of a crime or fraud that the lawyer reasonably believes is likely to result in death or serious bodily harm, or in substantial injury to the financial interests or property of another (ABA 1999:rule 1.6). In practice, the value of confidentiality is so dominant that lawyers often warn clients not to divulge such information so that the attorneys will have no need to violate the sanctity of lawyer-client communications.

When communicating with lawyers, social workers may become frustrated by the lack of information and dialogue. Lawyers often seem to be controlling the interview with questions, without divulging any information in return. Once again, social workers can improve their working relationships with lawyers if they view this interaction from the perspective of the lawyer, who must maintain vigilance about a client's confidences; social workers are much more effective in dealing with lawyers if they understand the need to secure specific releases and that the reluctance of lawyers to freely share client information is a means of protecting important client rights. The ABA's rules explain the lawyer's duty clearly: A lawyer should act with commitment and dedication to the interests of the client and with zeal in advocacy upon the client's behalf (1999:rule 1.3).

ZEALOUS ADVOCACY. Ethical consideration 7-19 of the ABA's 1981 *Model Code of Professional Responsibility* articulated well the duty of the lawyer to the adversary system of justice:

> Our legal system provides for the adjudication of disputes governed by the rules of substantive, evidentiary, and procedural law. An adversary presenta-

tion counters the natural human tendency to judge too swiftly in terms of the familiar that which is not yet fully known; the advocate, by his zealous preparation and presentation of facts and law, enables the tribunal to come to the hearing with an open and neutral mind and to render impartial judgments.

Currently, the legal profession is facing a crisis of professionalism, as reflected in three common observations about it: the public is dissatisfied with lawyers, lawyers are dissatisfied with other lawyers, and many lawyers are dissatisfied with being lawyers (Gaetke 1998). The temptation is to dismiss the duty of a lawyer to provide zealous representation as nothing more than a convenient excuse for boorish, bullying behavior. Legal advocacy is a complex duty, however, demanding a balanced examination of the costs and benefits to the legal profession, clients, and society.

Access to zealous and competent lawyers is critical for disenfranchised groups and disempowered individual clients in order to challenge the entrenched power of government or corporations. Society has created a stereotype of attorneys that highlights the dark side of the law while failing to give enough attention to the good done for society by a legal system that allows the less powerful to compete against more powerful interests on an even playing field.

Critics of the adversarial process point to the narrow interpretation, to which most lawyers subscribe, of what constitutes zealous representation (Tesler 1999). In many legal matters, especially those related to family and mental health law, the adversarial process can exacerbate problems, causing iatrogenic harm to a vulnerable client or family member. The experience of receiving legal help actually causes harm to the client. Why is it that the power of the adversarial model persists, even when the evidence is clear that it does not always work?

One answer may be in the personalities of lawyers as a group. People who are drawn to the law tend to be logical and most comfortable with outcomes that are measurable and least comfortable with the emotional and relational aspects of a client's life (Tesler 1999). Research has shown that lawyers appear to be more competitive and aggressive than most adults, more likely to seek dominance in interpersonal interactions and more driven to succeed. Further, lawyers tend to focus on objective analysis, with less orientation to human, emotional, and interpersonal concerns (Daicoff 1997).

Barnhizer (2000) argues convincingly that an important social benefit results from a lawyer's aggressive approach and commitment to the professional mission of providing zealous and competent representation to the client. He captures the ambiguity of the lawyer's role as simultaneously a "prince of darkness" and an "angel of light." The former description characterizes the lawyer as a manipulator of people and systems, while the latter description recognizes the lawyer as a heroic figure, championing the cause of underdog clients.

Barnhizer acknowledges the need for reforms but cautions against abandoning the benefits to society of a well-functioning adversarial system. His central thesis is that the use of the "dark skills" by lawyers to manipulate systems and gain power is a necessary part of being a good lawyer and an important reason why U.S. democracy works. However, the use of dark skills extracts a price: increased social enmity for the profession, as well as the increased dissatisfaction of many lawyers with the practice of law.

Rather than broadly decrying the use of zealous representation and the gladiator style of practice (Tesler 1999), the reforms of the 1990s—including the increased use of alternative dispute resolution, collaborative and preventive law practice, and therapeutic jurisprudence—suggest that an alternative paradigm is emerging for preparing lawyers to practice. The role assumed by a lawyer should depend on the context and the purpose of the legal action. For example, when the purpose of a legal intervention is to protect civil rights, to champion social causes, or to protect a client from a civil or criminal complaint, the role of zealous advocate is warranted and desirable. When the purpose of a legal intervention is to prevent legal problems, the lawyer may assume the advisory role of counselor-at-law. When the purpose of a legal intervention is to manage the legal needs of families going through life transitions, the most effective legal role may be a collaborative, interdisciplinary approach. Many family law cases have no winners and losers, so lawyers need to think in a way that is different from the traditional adversarial approach (J. Rosenberg 2000). The collaborative approach may not be possible where the power differential among parties is large or where violence or other abuse has been present. Social workers can improve the legal experience of clients by forging productive working relationships with attorneys who understand the need to match their approach to the needs of the client.

PROFESSIONAL PREPARATION AND COMPETENCE. The Socratic questioning techniques of many law professors, as made famous by the actor John Houseman in the *Paper Chase*, inculcates law students with the need for thorough preparation. The prospect of being called upon to answer questions about a single case (of the many cases assigned for each class) can be intimidating and perversely motivating. Junior associates of law firms are often expected to do the legal research that partners use in advising a client or litigating a case. Promotion and pay raises depend on the quality and thoroughness of the legal research. Once in practice, lawyers are part of the advocacy system, which creates a climate of competition among lawyers that reinforces the need for professional preparation and competence. In addition, judges often ask specific questions in oral arguments concerning how a particular case or statute applies to the case in question. Appearing in court or preparing a legal brief without a thorough knowledge of the law is unthinkable for most lawyers.

The core commodity that a lawyer provides is information. Lawyers can represent a client's interests and advise a course of action only if their legal information is grounded in a current understanding of the law. The central focus of providing legal advice is prevention of harm and/or damage control (Samar 1998). Society, the legal system, and the profession expect lawyers to have a basic understanding of the law and to undertake legal research in relation to the particular facts of a case. However, legal research provides information only about the text of the law and how it has been applied in the past. Research may not be as effective for determining what the law may be in the future or how a particular case might be decided. The lawyer may have to examine social trends and legal developments in other areas to make an informed judgment about the client's legal rights or liabilities. To effectively counsel clients and represent their interests, lawyers must undertake an exceptionally high level of preparation.

Legal education is oriented around a set of core fields that provide a lawyer with a general foundation. As lawyers gain practice experience, they tend to specialize in particular areas of the law. An attorney with a general practice may be able to handle common legal needs such as real estate closings, wills, probate matters, and simple criminal charges. It takes years for lawyers to develop the level of expertise that makes them specialists in a particular area of law. Just as in social work practice, lawyers have a responsibility to accept a case only when they are capable of handling the matter competently (ABA 1999:rule 1.1).

Finally, competence includes the responsibility of the lawyer not to neglect a legal matter (ABA 1999:rule 1.3). Lawyers must maintain a precise calendar and responsibly follow through on all matters related to representing a client. Legal procedures are governed by specific requirements, such as the number of days given to file legal motions or appeals with a court or administrative agency, and the statutory time limits for filing lawsuits.

Social workers may have little patience for lawyers' delays in returning telephone calls, and clients may not be able to get a question answered in a timely fashion. The day-to-day reality of legal practice is that lawyers sometimes do not have enough time to respond to the needs of every client. A client in crisis may consume an entire day. Scheduled court appearances may conflict with a lawyer's participation in a trial that goes longer than expected. As social workers, we know about such demands on our schedules and can be empathetic with these circumstances. Still, lawyers must be mindful of their responsibility to communicate with clients in a timely manner and to perform all duties concerning their legal representation. Social workers must be vigilant advocates for clients who need to communicate with their lawyers.

SCIENCE AND ART IN LEGAL PRACTICE

Social workers often remark that effective practice combines art and science (Sheafor, Horejsi, and Horejsi 1991). The same is true for lawyers who see the competition in presenting evidence, telling the story, and eloquently presenting well-reasoned arguments as the practice of a craft.

Competent lawyers combine technical knowledge of the law and creative skills for legal practice. Among the skills that are valuable, perhaps none is more significant than the ability to organize and categorize one's thinking process. Lawyers must be able to listen to a set of facts and determine the legal classification of a case. In the law this is called issue spotting. The examples that follow demonstrate its significance.

A city attorney is responsible for representing municipal agencies and employees. The city's youth services agency has received a request from a woman to release a copy of the clinical records of her seventeen-year-old son's individual counseling, as well as records from family counseling sessions. She has been threatening to sue if the agency does not release the records. The social worker is concerned that the son's records contain sensitive information about his drug use and sexual behavior that the youth wants to remain private. The city's lawyer, recognizing the variety of legal issues, begins by examining state statutes related to medical records, privileged communication, treatment of minors, parent's rights, and rules of evidence. He reviews federal statutes governing alcohol and drug treatment records. He calls on local experts to determine the professional social work standards related to the release of a minor's records. With this preparation he contacts the woman's attorney to negotiate a partial release of information that would satisfy the law while protecting the rights of the son.

A group of agency social workers is sitting around a table complaining about their agency's proposal alter to their work schedule to include coverage of evening hours. Their discussion focuses on how to comply with the new requirement. An attorney who is listening to the conversation immediately asks about the employee handbook and the type of contract that the workers have with the agency. She is homing in on the essential legal question concerning the contractual rights of the administration and the workers.

Once a lawyer has classified a set of facts into a legal question, the skills of applying a logical thought process to the case become prominent. The ability to present a clear and persuasive argument, both in written and spoken form, is the most recognized art of the lawyer. Many lawyers speak as if their skill can compensate for the weaknesses in a case. However, evidence that this is true is inconclusive (Schrager 1999). In many cases a good lawyer could argue the same facts in both directions. A skilled lawyer will anticipate the opposing argument and attempt to present a logical counterargument. Being effective in legal discourse requires discipline, organized thinking, and analytical skills.

The art of legal practice includes the ability to relate the narrative of a client in a way that moves the legal system to action. A good lawyer is an effective storyteller. Recently, legal scholars have begun to look at law as the stories of people's lives. Law stories, by their very nature, are complex and compelling dramas, and they are played out in an environment that has its own idiosyncratic culture, processes, and language (P. Brooks and Gerwitz 1996). The heavy media coverage of notorious legal cases bears out the power of these narratives. How are these stories constructed and communicated? What are the dynamics of the interactions among litigants, lawyers, judges, and witnesses? Telling stories is especially significant for those groups that traditionally have less power—women, sexual minorities, persons of color, and children. If their voices, emotions, and experiences have a platform, the narratives of these individuals can provide an opportunity to break through simplistic thinking (McKinnon 1996).

Social workers seeking to understand the law can begin with a reminder that a personal story is behind every legal case. One of the greatest opportunities for influence lies in what social workers can do to help the legal system and the public to hear these narratives. Traditional legal analysis and argumentation often do not reflect the felt needs and experiences of the injured or aggrieved person. The training of lawyers, to focus on specific legal elements of a case, may result in a client's feeling unheard. Often the lawyer and client struggle over which reality will define the case. In the legal setting the dominant narrative may invalidate the experiences of unequal groups. Their story, effectively communicated, can have infinitely more persuasive force than a volume full of statistics.

INTRODUCTION TO LEGAL REASONING

Levi describes the classic view of legal reasoning: a lawyer begins by identifying similarities between a current legal case and a previously decided case and then analyzes the rule of law that the judge applied in the decided case. Finally, the lawyer argues that this rule of law should be applied to the current case (1949). Although this statement captures the essence of analogical reasoning (comparing cases or rules that bear some resemblance to each other or share some characteristic), it is only one part of how legal reasoning operates in practice.

Legal scholarship has overemphasized the role of classic legal reasoning. Analogical reasoning has an important role to play in cases that are being tried in court, but only a small percentage of legal matters is resolved in a formal court hearing. Even when the judge makes a decision during a formal hearing, the lawyers often have negotiated this determination before the actual trial. Engaging in a structured legal analysis allows a lawyer to consider all aspects of a client's situation, and its use is fundamental to understanding the thought process and actions of an attorney.

Lawyers seek the meaning of legal rules and principles to argue for an outcome in their client's best interests. They use logic and rhetoric to advance their argument. Vandevelde argues that analogical reasoning and the goal of a particular case guide the thought process of a lawyer. He identifies the five steps that a lawyer should take in the legal reasoning process:

1. Identify the sources of law (statutes, cases, regulations) that apply to the factual situation.
2. Analyze the sources of law to determine the applicable rules of law and the policies underlying those rules.
3. Synthesize the rules into a coherent structure in which the more specific rules are grouped under the more general ones.

4. Research the available facts.
5. Apply the structure of rules to the facts to ascertain the rights and duties of the parties, using the underlying policies to resolve difficult cases. (1998:2)

The analysis begins with a complete gathering of the facts. A detail that might seem trivial could be determinative of a legal right. The lawyer then undertakes a review of statutory and common law rules to assess the various rights and duties of a client. Many lawyers use a type of decision-making tree to identify the specific legal issues and the possible remedies to benefit the client. Does the case involve contract law? Has someone committed a tort (private harm) such as negligence or libel? Does a statute or administrative regulation address the issue? Do the facts mean that the client could face criminal charges or an administrative complaint? What might be the negative consequences for the client of limiting other legal options? What is the potential for recovering monetary damages? How will the client pay for the legal services? These and other questions structure the thinking of an attorney and help to determine whether to refer the client to a specialist or to a free legal clinic or to accept the case and prepare a strategy to protect the interests of the client.

JEROME

Jerome was an experienced clinician with a small private clinical social work practice. He worked ten hours a week for a local agency that provided social services to people with HIV. In this role Jerome ran a couple of groups and saw some individual clients. The agency director had approached Jerome six months earlier, asking him to supervise George, a newly hired caseworker. George had no professional degree but was great with clients and connected to the community. Because Jerome's contracted hours were full, he arranged to have the new worker come to his private office for weekly supervision, for which he would be paid an hourly rate.

After the first three supervision sessions, Jerome suspected that the new worker would have problems. George seemed unable to separate his personal feelings from his professional decisions. Still, Jerome was shocked during their fourth meeting when George admitted that he had engaged in a consensual sexual act with an adult client in the office bathroom. Jerome was frightened that he would be liable for the acts of his supervisee. He was not sure whether he owed any duty of confidentiality to George not to divulge the information to the agency. Jerome called a lawyer for consultation.

Following Vandevelde's steps, Jerome's lawyer might engage in the follow-ing process. First, after listening to the basic facts and asking clarifying ques-tions, the lawyer would consider the applicable sources of law, and in this case he would begin with the criminal statutes. Some states have made it a crime for counselors to engage in sexual relations with clients (e.g., Conn. Gen. Stat. 53a–71 [1997]). The lawyer would need to recall or research the language of the law, as well as any cases decided under the law, to determine its coverage. Does the law extend only to licensed professionals? Does it apply to those who work under the supervision of a licensed professional? Is it applicable only to inpa-tient units? Does the client have to be impaired and thus unable to consent? Is the intent of the law to protect mental health patients from being raped by those entrusted to care for them?

A second area of law that the lawyer must analyze governs the supervision relationship. Here the issue is whether the client could sue the supervisor for professional negligence. In other words, should the supervisor have known that this was occurring, and did the supervisor have an opportunity to prevent the harm? Statutes and regulations may not address these issues directly, so the lawyer would need to rely on two sources of law. First, do any cases detail the duties of a supervisor? Second, what are the professional standards for supervi-sion in social work? In answering the first question, the lawyer would seek to de-termine whether courts in the jurisdiction have determined whether a supervi-sor owes a duty to the client of a supervisee, even if the supervisor never has seen the client personally. In answering the second question, the lawyer would compare the actions of Jerome with reasonable professional behavior for social work supervisors. The lawyer also would need to examine state statutes on priv-ileged communication and confidentiality to determine whether Jerome owed any duty to George to keep the information shared in supervision confidential.

When lawyers define a legal rule, they use analogies to determine how they might treat certain facts (Sunstein 1996). Jerome's lawyer might ask whether case law has held a superior liable for the actions of subordinates. If it has not, the lawyer next would research the case law to find situations that share char-acteristics of this supervisory relationship.

For example, the lawyer may find a case in which a pizza restaurant was found to be liable for the actions of a delivery driver who drove recklessly and caused an accident. The rulings may have found that the restaurant's guarantee of hot pizza created the condition under which the harm was likely to occur. In Jerome's case, was anything about his behavior analogous to the hot pizza guar-antee? Did Jerome counsel George to become close to his clients without ex-plaining boundary violations to him? Did Jerome allow a nonprofessional to work with clients in a capacity that demanded an experienced clinician? The analogical reasoning process structures the legal argument: Case A was decided based on principle X. Case B resembles case A. Therefore, principle X is likely to determine the result in case B. In order to maintain consistency of legal principles, justice demands that we decide like cases in like ways (Sunstein 1996).

An additional issue might involve the status of Jerome in relationship to the agency. Depending on insurance coverage, determining whether Jerome was working as an employee or an independent contractor when providing the supervision to George may prove important to this case. Jerome's malpractice carrier might seek to argue that it bears no responsibility for the case because the supervision was connected to Jerome's job at the agency. Therefore, the entire focus of Jerome's lawyer initially might be to resolve this question because it may determine whether Jerome would be implicated in a lawsuit arising from this situation.

The lawyer also would consider other issues in preparing to advise Jerome about his liabilities and responsibilities. This case illustrates the way that legal reasoning unfolds. Generally, the daily practice of law is not about big principles and policy change. It is about undertaking a disciplined, organized thought process with the goal of protecting the interests of a client. Criticizing an attorney for not articulating the exact parameters of the law is easy. However, studying legal reasoning and legal practice makes clear that a lawyer's challenge is to apply existing law to the facts in order to get the best possible result for the client. In most cases, even where the law does not appear to be supportive, a lawyer is expected to construct an argument as to why a judge should accept the proffered rationale for distinguishing this situation from the established law. This is the process within which the law evolves while remaining substantially predictable.

LEGAL KNOWLEDGE FOR SOCIAL WORKERS

Nam et ipsa scientia potestas est. (For knowledge itself is power.)

—Sir Francis Bacon

If social workers are to strive for legal literacy, one psychological hurdle that they must overcome is the idea that law and social work practice are different things. As I stated at the beginning of chapter 1, law governs all social work practice to some degree. Social workers regularly apply legal rules to their practice, for example, when they abide by the requirement to obtain informed consent before treatment and when they honor the mandate to report abuse involving children. Social workers also contribute to legal decisions by providing opinions to courts that influence the legal status of a dependent client. In a variety of social service settings, social workers use the discretion granted to them by statute or administrative regulation to determine eligibility for benefits and services (Gaskins 1981).

Social workers regularly use legal thinking and apply legal rules in practice. Obviously, social workers can manage legal issues better if they think about what they are doing (Read 1986). Naive expectations about the law frequently frustrate social workers in their pursuit of legal knowledge. The law offers no precise guidance for many legal questions that arise in day-to-day social work practice. Yet social workers want a definitive response from the law. Is it legal for me to withhold treatment records from a client? What are my legal obligations to inform an adolescent client's parents of their teen's drug use? Is it legal for a child welfare worker to remove a newborn from the care of a mother who was convicted of child abuse ten years earlier? The generic answer to all these questions is a decidedly legal, hedged response: It depends. Rather than seeking definitive answers about specific issues, social workers need to understand the parameters of authority that the law explicitly and implicitly grants to professionals. With this legal knowledge social workers can practice in a more legally competent manner.

PROFESSIONAL JUDGMENT AND LEGAL DISCRETION

Discretion is a concept central to understanding professional authority to apply legal rules. The most important outlines of discretionary authority may be found in professional, ethical, and practice standards, as well as statutes governing social programs. Professional guidelines, ethical codes and current research on best practices for various clinical areas articulate the standards of care for social workers. Social workers in all settings have a duty to know these standards and to act in a professionally competent and responsible manner. The legal system grants social workers the authority to make practice decisions as long as they fall within professional standards of care. The legal system also enforces these practice standards through malpractice lawsuits and state social work licensing boards. As a result, social work practice standards have become the legal standards by which a social worker's actions are evaluated.

In clinical social work settings, among the many legal rules are those mandating the reporting of abuse and delineating the duty to warn of a threat of harm, the duty to maintain confidentiality, the duty not to engage in fraudulent practices, and the duty to maintain proper business records. In child welfare settings legal rules outline the investigative process and the standards to be used for decision making. Social workers also must follow due process procedures, as well as court orders and protocols, in each case. In social work practice with elderly populations, legal rules protect the rights and safety of those who need assistance in managing their affairs and making decisions. In court settings social workers who are employed by probation and public defender offices must practice within the legal rules of criminal procedure, attorney-client privilege, and court supervision, among other legal guidelines.

Laws and regulations can influence the professional discretion of social workers. For example, consider the case of geriatric social workers who exercise professional discretion to secure health-care resources for their clients. What are the values that influence these practice decisions? Are any values stated in any laws or regulations that can provide insight for the practitioner? The value of self-determination has emerged in statutes and administrative regulations as a fundamental one, to be preserved and enhanced in both home- and community-based services. For example, virtually all client bills of rights embody this principle in some form (Kapp 1996). Social workers who recognize and act from the implicit or explicit values of a legal rule can be confident that the legal system will support their resulting practice decisions.

To what degree does the legal system allow a social worker to exercise professional discretion? In what circumstances are courts likely to second-guess the decisions of a social worker? In the absence of specific legal rules or testimony from an expert that the social worker's actions did not meet professional standards, courts generally assume that a social worker has exercised sound professional discretion (*Youngblood v. Romeo* [1982]). For those practice situations where explicit legal rules apply, courts or administrative agencies may review the professional's actions to determine whether the worker followed procedural and substantive elements of the legal rule.

The judicial system's treatment of professional discretion has changed over time. Mosher (1987) points out that public agencies became increasingly identified with, and dominated by, the professions, including social work, after World War II. However, professional norms, values, and standards governed these professions more than did the directives of administrative regulations or statutes. Clinical decisions based on professional judgment were relatively secure because courts traditionally hesitated to second-guess experts who had the training and expertise in the area under question.

During the civil rights movement legal advocates for vulnerable populations began to challenge professional discretion. They based these challenges on the perception that social workers and other professionals exercised too much discretion, resulting in paternalistic and uneven decisions that denied civil rights to some populations (Gaskins 1981). For example, in the field of mental health clinical assessments of clients provided the legal justification for involuntary hospitalization. Lawyers, concerned about the lack of accountability for such evaluations, worked for increased judicial review of professional decisions (Tyler 1992).

In the late 1960s welfare programs became increasingly rule based. Before that time a social work model was the basis for running the programs, and it left critical decisions to the professional discretion of case workers (Diller 2000). In the absence of formal rules the decisions of a welfare agency were difficult to challenge because they rested on professional judgment. As the welfare system became increasingly rule based, lawyers turned to the courts to challenge these procedures (that is, the lawyers sought evidence that welfare agencies followed due process procedures in terminating welfare benefits) (*Goldberg v. Kelly* [1970]).

In the context of prison settings, courts have deferred to health-care professionals to decide what services the state should provide to prisoners. A prisoner sued prison officials for denying care that medical professionals had recommended. The Supreme Court ruled that the denial constituted deliberate indifference to the needs of the prisoner. The Court based its decision on the recognition that the professional judgment of the health-care provider is more important than the cost concerns that had led state prison officials to deny the prisoner the medical services (*Estelle v. Gamble* [1976]).

The exercise of professional discretion has not always led to positive results for society. Smith (1991) has argued that the discretionary judgments of legal professionals often result in discriminatory outcomes for poor and disenfranchised populations. Lipsky (1987) advanced the classic argument that those professionals who have direct contact with clients exercise broad discretion in applying legal rules. Consider a recent example of the abuse of professional discretion. Traffic stops by police that target members of particular racial groups have generated considerable controversy. Constitutional law sets the legal standard for when police may stop a motor vehicle. The officer must have a reasonable suspicion that the driver has been, or is about to be, involved in criminal activity or must have a reasonable safety concern about the operation of the motor vehicle (*State v. Hopper* [1996]).

Racial profiling occurs when police target someone for investigation on the basis of that person's race, national origin, or ethnicity. Examples of profiling are the use of race to determine which drivers to stop for minor traffic violations (often derisively called driving while black), and the use of race to determine which motorists or pedestrians to search for contraband (Harris 1999). The issue has galvanized public anger and focused attention on police discretion. In the case of racial profiling, the challenges to police discretion have resulted in new procedures to limit the discretion of professional law enforcement officers and to reinforce the legal rules governing traffic stops.

The essential issue for social workers is to determine when and to what extent a court or other legal authority would grant them the discretion to make professional decisions in applying legal rules. The analysis has two prongs. First, in an effort to restrict arbitrary use of professional authority, such as involuntary commitment or termination of public benefits, courts apply a procedural due process test: Were all the procedures followed, providing clients with a fair and just process, an opportunity to be heard, and adequate protection of their rights? Social workers need to ensure that clients' rights are protected through agency adherence to consistent, unbiased, and open processes. The added benefit of this type of process is that clients feel that they have been treated fairly and are more positive about the professional decision, regardless of the outcome (Tyler 1992).

Social workers unfamiliar with basic legal guidelines face the daunting task of applying legal rules without knowing the content of those rules. As a result, social workers may be anxious in practice or defend their ignorance by denying the significance of legal mandates. How do courts evaluate the substantive elements of social work practice decisions? The courts recognize social work practice as an inexact science. For example, New York's highest court established a professional judgment standard in *Schrempf v. State* (1985) that allows therapists some flexibility in making clinical decisions based on individual client considerations. This standard concedes the difficulty in evaluating professional decisions in the mental health arena, especially after a tragedy has occurred.

Courts generally acknowledge the need to respect the judgment of professionals, including social workers. If a question arises about the substantive decisions of a social worker, the legal standard is whether the conduct of the professional fell below the minimum level of care for the profession such that it constituted recklessness, gross negligence, or deliberate indifference. In other words, the analysis determines whether the professional's subjective response was so inadequate that it demonstrated an absence of professional judgment (*Steele v. Choi* [1996]; *Collignon v. Milwaukee County* [1998]).

But courts sometimes do not respect professional judgments in specific decisions. When judges or other legal officials disagree with the professional judgment of social workers, the officials are exercising the discretionary power allocated to the judiciary. Viewing this in the most favorable light, judicial discretion acts as a check on whether a social worker's judgment was based on proper application of the legal rule and whether the social worker respected the client's due process rights.

In some cases, however, judges make highly questionable decisions that seem to obviate the tradition of deferring to professional standards. At times, because of arrogance or ignorance, courts or administrative agencies will substitute their judgment for the judgment of a professional without the requisite proof of any substantive or procedural deficiencies.

- A protective services social worker uses her discretion to remove a child from a chaotic family situation, only to have a judge minimize the concerns raised in the worker's affidavit and return the child to the home.
- A clinical social worker decides not to inform the parents of a reluctant thirteen-year-old client about the extent of their son's drug use. At a hearing after the youth dies of an overdose, the state licensing board finds the social worker should have informed the parents.
- A social worker's report details the poor fit between the needs of the client and the ability of the program to meet those needs. The program provides vocational services to people with cognitive disabilities, but the client's mental health difficulties tax the ability of the staff to monitor his safety. Still, the judge, acting on a motion from the client's lawyer, issues a temporary restraining order prohibiting the program from terminating the client.

As social workers continue to develop empirically validated practice approaches and standards, and as social workers learn about the legal rules that guide practice, evidence of compliance with the law will make courts more inclined to uphold professional discretion.

Social workers have no guarantee that judges will support their professional judgments in all cases. When social workers base their practice decisions on empirically validated treatment approaches and follow professional standards of care, courts usually will not second-guess their decisions. However, as I have described in this chapter, the practice of law involves lawyers and judges in a complex process of resolving disputes. When a decision in an individual case does not support a social worker's judgment, the decision must be regarded in the context of the adversarial system.

5.

THE LITIGATION PROCESS: DISSECTING A COURT CASE

Strange enlightenments are vouchsafed for those who seek higher places.
—Flann O'Brien, *The Third Policeman*

PEOPLE OFTEN think of the litigation process as what occurs in a courtroom during a trial. However, the dramatic images that emerge from movies, television, and novels are like the visible part of an iceberg. Most of the substance is below the surface. These invisible layers of the legal process contain some barriers to the legal system. If a dispute reaches the legal system, the parties can settle or stall the case at a number of points. Social workers must appreciate the complete process of litigation in order to play an active role at the most influential moments in the life of a legal case.

The first potential impediment faced by a person involved in a dispute is gaining access to the legal system. In a criminal case a defendant has a constitutional right to legal representation and a trial by jury. Getting other types of cases to court also may be a right, but if a person has limited wealth and education, or if other factors such as language or transportation block access to courts, that person may need an advocate to break through the barriers (Winfield 1995). As I discuss throughout this book, complex language and procedures characterize legal systems. Most people need a lawyer to navigate most legal systems, but unless they can afford hourly fees, access to legal help may be difficult to obtain. Cutbacks in federal funding of legal services for the poor have reduced the opportunity for low-cost legal assistance (McNeal 2001), and Republicans have tried to restrict the types of legal advocacy practiced by government-funded legal services (*Legal Services Corporation v. Velazquez* [2001]). As a result, many populations served by social workers have limited access to legal representation and therefore to the courts.

If a case reaches the legal system, a trial court may hear the dispute. This is the stage at which most cases are exposed to the public. Public policy requires most court proceedings to be open to the public and press. Exceptions to this rule include family and juvenile court proceedings, where hearings are generally closed. Accountability and confidence in the legal system increase when the citizenry has an opportunity to observe the workings of the court and scrutinize the fairness of the participants and procedures (Winfield 1995). However, many legal cases never get to court. The pretrial processes, alternative dispute-resolution strategies, plea bargaining in criminal cases, and pretrial negotiation can resolve a legal dispute before it reaches the courts. While this may be a positive result in that it avoids the time, cost, and angst of litigation, some social costs result when the outcome of the case is kept private. For example, confidential settlements often do not require the liable party to acknowledge public responsibility, and the case may not establish any new legal rights.

The benefits of an open process accrue to the individual litigants as well as the public. People who experience the court system as fair generally have had the opportunity to participate in the process, have been treated with dignity and respect by legal professionals, and assess the motivations of the court as being trustworthy (Tyler 1992). Faith in the legal system contributes to social order by reinforcing the idea that the legal system can resolve individual grievances. An excellent example of the confidence that the American public has in the judiciary is the social and political order following the Supreme Court's decision in the 2000 presidential election (*Bush v. Gore* [2000]).

THE STAGES OF A LAWSUIT OR CRIMINAL TRIAL

Access to legal systems, accountability of legal results, and the credibility of litigation processes are the essential issues for social workers to understand in order to be effective advocates and participants in lawsuits. The process of litigation can be confusing, and the rationale behind the procedures may seem arcane. However, civil and criminal procedures have a logic that protects the rights of the plaintiff, the rights of the defendant, and the legitimacy of the legal system.

In this chapter I will explore the stages of a lawsuit by tracing the path of a case brought against a social worker, beginning with the complaint and continuing through the ultimate resolution. I will describe the basic stages and the purpose of the lawyers' actions at each stage. Every case presents unique issues and the description that follows is admittedly oversimplified. In addition, the terminology varies by court and jurisdiction, so it may not match every experience. The purpose is to highlight the skeletal framework of complex litigation processes.

CORA V. MARY

Mary, a clinical social worker with a solo private practice, began to see Cora in treatment one year ago. At that time Cora was transferring from a therapist she had seen for eight years. This therapist had closed her practice because of her failing health. The referral information described Cora as manipulative and a person who had difficulties in relationships. Her diagnosis was borderline personality disorder. She also had a history of arrests for violent and aggressive behavior. After several sessions Mary referred Cora to a local psychiatrist for a medication evaluation. The psychiatrist prescribed medication and arranged for a monthly appointment to monitor Cora's progress.

The therapeutic relationship between Cora and Mary grew increasingly intense. Cora became demanding and Mary responded by agreeing to see Cora twice a week. Cora frequently left messages with Mary's answering service between sessions. She would report that she was in crisis, and on several occasions she expressed suicidal ideation. Cora became angry with Mary when confronted, verbally berating her clinical skills, comparing Mary unfavorably to her former therapist. Mary was concerned that these episodes of anger were becoming more frequent and more threatening. Cora began to write a series of letters to Mary during this time. The final letter contained abusive language and veiled references to harming Mary and her family. "Be careful, I heard that the brakes in Honda Accords tend to fail a lot." "Your daughter has such pretty blonde hair, I hope she is alright."

Mary was frightened by the threats and assessed Cora as capable of carrying them out. After consulting with her peer supervision group, she informed the psychiatrist of her intent to end treatment with Cora because of the safety concerns and the effect of the threats on the treatment relationship. The psychiatrist agreed to increase his sessions with Cora until she found a new therapist. Mary decided that an extended termination process would likely result in a dramatic reaction, including escalating suicidal or threatening behaviors by Cora. Mary decided to terminate the treatment immediately and informed Cora at the next session that the therapy was not productive and that she no longer was willing to provide services. She informed Cora of the availability of the psychiatrist for interim therapy and provided her with a list of several local therapists.

Cora left the office in a rage, and six days later she attempted suicide by ingesting a large quantity of prescription drugs. Cora was hospitalized and may have lasting brain damage from the overdose. She is receiving physical therapy in a rehabilitation hospital. Mary learned about the suicide attempt when

Cora's parents contacted her and said that they had been appointed Cora's guardian by the probate court. They also said they had retained an attorney and were planning to sue her for abandonment and malpractice.

PRELIMINARIES

A number of activities at the beginning of a legal controversy determine the future of the case. Let us assume that Cora's family has hired a competent attorney who accepts the case conditionally, pending a review of the factual and legal bases for a lawsuit. In criminal cases, and in civil complaints where the chance of winning a damage award is small, attorneys generally require a retainer, an initial fee to finance the activities of the case. In some matters attorneys may charge a flat fee, but more commonly they charge by the hour. The ethical lawyer provides a good-faith estimate of the total cost of the legal representation. In a case such as that presented by Cora's family, the attorney may accept the case on the basis of a contingency fee. If the parents win their case and the court awards damages, the attorney will take a percentage of the award as the legal fee (traditionally, one-third of the total, although this can vary according to the amount of work that the lawyer did before settlement or a decision and whether the percentage is calculated before or after expenses). If the parents lose their case, they owe the lawyer nothing.

Mary should consider retaining her own lawyer. As I discussed in chapter 4, her insurance company will assign an attorney to represent its interests. The insurance company would be responsible for paying damages if Mary loses the case. It may be that Mary's interests will be consistent with the insurance company's interests, but Mary should consider separate legal counsel to protect her rights during the process. Litigation is a lawyer's game and the attorneys retain most of the control of the technical processes. Mary needs to have an advocate speaking on her behalf as the malpractice insurance company makes decisions in the case.

PLEADINGS AND PRETRIAL DISCOVERY

The initial task of the lawyers is to conduct a preliminary investigation of the facts of the case, perhaps including interviews with the parties and the collection of Cora's clinical treatment records. This stage is called pretrial discovery.

Relying on an exception to the confidentiality and privilege laws, Mary is able to share Cora's records with her attorney so that she can defend herself from the lawsuit. The purpose of the initial fact finding is to determine whether Mary has a legal responsibility to pay any damages to Cora. The lawyer for Cora's family would need to examine professional negligence law as well as contract law to assess the duty that Mary owed to her client. Did Mary have a professional duty not to terminate treatment so abruptly? Did Mary have a professional duty to ensure the effective transfer of the case to another therapist before terminating the treatment? Did Mary have a contractual obligation to continue to provide treatment to Cora? If Mary did not meet any of these legal expectations, and Cora's parents could prove it in court, would Mary have to pay damages to Cora's parents? Does Mary share liability with any other parties such as the psychiatrist or members of her peer supervision group? If any question exists about whether the insurance coverage would pay for the full amount of the damages, the attorney representing Cora's parents could name in the suit any or all professionals who had a role in the case so that the parents could tap the professionals' insurance or assets.

The lawyer for Cora's parents would need to decide in which court to file the case. Suppose that Cora lives in one state and Mary's practice is in a neighboring state. Determining which court has jurisdiction, and whether either jurisdiction has legal rules or case law that favors one side or another, requires a complex legal analysis. The choice of jurisdiction can determine whether the case can proceed, so sometimes the legal fight about which court has jurisdiction is the most important issue in the case.

Court rules specify the length of time that a person has to file a lawsuit and the time that a state prosecutor has to file a criminal complaint. These restrictions, called statutes of limitation, vary by jurisdiction and by the type of case. The rationale for having a statute of limitations is twofold. Justice requires that cases be litigated in a timely manner when the evidence is fresh and the memory of witnesses is not diminished. In addition, as a public policy matter, allowing the accused to have their day in court within a reasonable time frame is important, rather than having the threat of potential litigation affect their ability to plan for their future.

For example, consider the possibility that the statute of limitations in state A is two years, whereas it is three years in neighboring state B. If Cora's parents file suit almost three years after her treatment ended, the case could be dismissed if it is deemed to be in the jurisdiction of state A. Her parents' lawyer would also need to determine the amount of damages to seek because some courts base their jurisdiction on the amount of money involved. The fight about which court has jurisdiction occurs during the pleading stage, but the research concerning these issues must be done before the case is filed.

After this initial research process the lawyer for Cora's parents would go to court to file the lawsuit with the court clerk. The case officially begins when the defendant is issued a summons identifying the names of the parties and providing notice of the complaint. A sheriff's deputy or process server delivers the summons and personally attests to the defendant's receipt of the documents. In response the defendant may make a motion to quash (invalidate) the summons on the ground that the court does not have jurisdiction or that the case is too old by legal standards.

The next stage of the process is often referred to as the pleadings stage. In the complaint the plaintiffs must state a legal claim that, if proved, would entitle them to recover damages. The lawyer for Cora's parents would present their (plaintiffs') version of the case in a structure that corresponds to elements of the legal rule. For example, the law of professional negligence requires professionals to practice in a manner consistent with the standard of care for similarly trained workers in similar professional settings. Further, the action of the professional must have caused the injury to the plaintiff. The parents' complaint might allege that Mary's abrupt termination of Cora's treatment was inconsistent with professional standards. Also, as a direct result of the abandonment by Mary, Cora's condition deteriorated, leading to her suicide attempt. Therefore, Mary should be held responsible for paying the damage to Cora arising from the act of professional negligence or malpractice. Note that the plaintiffs need not offer specific proof at this stage of the process. However, the complaint must state a claim that is legally sufficient under the substantive law. The lawyer must also follow technical procedural rules in preparing and filing the complaint.

The defendant's first line of defense is to attack the pleadings by making motions to the court. The defense attorney may argue that the plaintiff failed to follow one or more of the rules regarding the form of the complaint. In most jurisdictions a finding that the complaint is deficient in form leads to the filing of an amended complaint. The defendant can also object to the substance of the complaint. In this type of objection the defendant does not question the factual presentation by the plaintiff but instead argues that "even if everything you claim is true, it is still not sufficient to state a legal claim." Finally, the defendant may file a counterclaim, arguing that the plaintiff's actions caused the defendant to suffer damages.

What type of arguments could a defense lawyer make in response to a malpractice complaint against a social worker? Mary's lawyer might argue that professional negligence standards do not apply to social workers because they are not medical professionals. This reasoning suggests that the correct standard should have been ordinary negligence, that is, what a reasonable person would have done in the situation. The judge would have to rule on the applicability of professional negligence standards to social workers by examining the statutes and case law presented by both lawyers in legal briefs on the motion. In this case the substantive law is well established in most jurisdictions that professional standards of care exist for clinical social work practice (Madden 1998). Therefore, a motion to dismiss a case on this basis would not have a good chance of success.

If the initial motion to dismiss the case does not succeed, the defense will develop an answer to the complaint. Some facts will be uncontested, such as Cora's having been a client of Mary's or the dates of service. The answer will deny other parts of the complaint. And the defense may raise affirmative defenses, sometimes known as the "yes but" approach. Mary's attorney might argue that Cora's threatening behaviors obviated the usual expectation that termination be a more gradual and planned process. The defense lawyer may also argue as an affirmative defense that the case should be dismissed. The motion to dismiss based on the affirmative defense would cite the established case law holding that an outpatient treatment provider has limited control over a suicidal client's life and thus would be unable to prevent a suicide attempt.

While the pleading stage is underway, lawyers are also compiling information associated with the facts and legal merits of the case. This process is known as discovery. In addition to collecting documents related to the case, each lawyer will want to conduct a formal interview with the opposing party and important witnesses. These interviews, called depositions, generally take place in the lawyer's office in the presence of a court reporter so that they can be transcribed for trial preparation. The questioning helps to further define the issues of the case and allows the attorneys to prepare for specific challenges to evidence. In an effort to make the trial more efficient, the judge will hold a pretrial conference with the attorneys to further decide the issues to be litigated.

Mary could prepare for her deposition by understanding the elements of the complaints alleging professional negligence and breach of contract. This would enable her to anticipate the types of questions that the lawyer for Cora's parents will ask. For example, she might review her practice policies and the materials that she provides to clients at the intake session in preparation for questions about the client's expectation that the treatment would continue until a mutually decided termination. On the malpractice claim Mary might prepare to detail the threats that Cora made and her attempts to ensure that Cora had access to ongoing treatment after termination.

Unfortunately, many cases headed to court do not receive the type of preparation described here. In some cases social workers receive a subpoena to testify without any knowledge of the legal case and without any warning of what element of a case their testimony is intended to prove or disprove. This is more likely to happen in cases where the monetary stakes are not high, such as child custody hearings, minor criminal cases, and juvenile court proceedings. Social workers should seek preparation time with lawyers who call them as witnesses in order to respond in a professionally competent manner.

Once the pleadings are closed, the case is ready for trial. Both sides have developed and refined the legal and factual issues, and they usually know which elements of the case their opponent will contest in a trial, as well as the chances of winning a verdict. Many lawsuits settle at this stage because neither side wishes to spend the money it takes to litigate a case all the way through to a final decision. An experienced defense lawyer who assesses the case as having a small chance of success would agree to an exit strategy that costs the insurance provider a minimal sum. An experienced plaintiff's lawyer would recommend accepting a small settlement offer if the case does not have a sound basis for success.

PRELIMINARY INJUNCTIONS

In some cases lawyers seek a ruling from the court before trial. A request for a preliminary injunction is known as an "equitable remedy" and is granted by a judge only in special circumstances. A judge may issue a preliminary injunction if convinced that one side could suffer irreparable harm if the other party is not forced to refrain from some potentially injurious type of behavior and the first party has a reasonable chance of winning the lawsuit (*Roland Machinery v. Dresser Industries* [1984]). When one side goes before a judge to make a motion, the motion is known as an ex parte motion. Consider a case where a managed-care company issues new guidelines for coverage of mental health treatment. Consumers of this health plan could bring a legal challenge, claiming that the changes are illegal under state insurance law. These consumers could ask the judge to issue a temporary injunction prohibiting the managed-care company from implementing the changes until the court decides whether they comply with the law. In this way the company could not deny coverage of mental health services to clients while the case was being litigated. The judge would look for compelling evidence documenting irreparable harm to those who did not receive treatment coverage. In addition, the judge would be likely to issue such an order if the evidence suggests that the consumers' suit is likely to succeed.

TRIAL

The trial court has two primary areas of responsibility. First, the court will seek clarity about the facts of the case. The trier of fact—either the jury or in some cases the judge—will determine which is the more persuasive version of what happened by listening to and evaluating the evidence. The second task of the trial court, specifically the judge, is to determine what legal rules should govern the case (Dernbach and Singleton 1981). Finally, the court reaches a decision and determines what the remedy or penalty will be if liability is determined.

Most cases like *Cora v. Mary* are tried in front of a jury. Either side has the right to ask for a trial by jury except for those cases in which the rules of the court do not allow for a jury, such as family court matters (because of the sensitive nature of the proceedings) and requests for injunctions (court orders prohibiting an activity). When the judge hears the evidence, the proceeding is known as a bench trial. In these cases the role of the judge is both to make a finding of fact and to apply the law to the facts.

In some cases the parties must submit to a mandatory dispute resolution procedure before a case can proceed to trial. The use of mediation, arbitration, and other alternative processes has been effective in encouraging settlements to avoid litigation and reduce the burden on overcrowded court dockets (Nelson 2000).

JURY SELECTION. Jury selection is the process by which lawyers and judges seek to ensure that a fair and unbiased group of citizens is assembled to hear a case. The people summoned to court on a particular day become part of the jury pool. From the larger group the clerk assembles jury panels to be considered for each case requiring a jury. In most courts the number of jurors needed for a case is twelve, although some courts use as few as six.

The lawyers or, in some jurisdictions, the judges interview each potential juror to determine whether any factor might create bias or conflict in ruling on the case. For example, in death penalty cases they ask potential jurors whether they could vote for a death sentence if the defendant is found guilty and meets the statutory criteria. The process of questioning the jurors is called voir dire. Lawyers may use two mechanisms to seek the exclusion of a citizen from participating in a case. First, the lawyer may challenge a potential juror for cause if that person has a bias or conflict that would call into question the ability to be neutral and objective in deciding a case. Second, lawyers have a number of peremptory challenges, which allow them to excuse a potential juror without stating the cause. Lawyers generally do this to construct a panel of jurors that they believe will be sympathetic to their side. Once the requisite number of jurors is impaneled, the jury is sworn in and the case can begin.

OPENING STATEMENTS. Before any evidence is presented, the plaintiff, or the prosecutor in a criminal case, provides a summary of the case. The opening statement generally outlines the factual basis of the litigation and reveals the lawyer's theory of the case by briefly discussing the legal issues and the type of proof to be offered. The defendant's lawyer generally makes an opening statement immediately after the plaintiff/prosecutor's but may choose to wait until after the opposing side has presented all its evidence. Experienced trial lawyers know that it is important to articulate themes that help a judge and jury to synthesize the evidence and formulate an opinion about the outcome (Schultz 2000). The opening statement provides the opportunity to set up the narrative of the case.

THEMES. The lawyer for Cora's family is likely to pursue the theme of abandonment of a person in need. The narrative of the case from this perspective would set forth the unqualified responsibility of a mental health professional to be loyal to a client in need, rather than responding with hysterical overreactions to manifestations of the client's diagnosis. The lawyer could argue, for example, that this unprofessional response resulted from a lack of understanding of the treatment of borderline personality disorder and insufficient clinical supervision—constituting professional negligence. The retrospective analysis of the duty of a social worker when an injury has occurred to a client is difficult to refute. A skillful presentation of the narrative oversimplifies the issues, pointing out how easy it would have been for the social worker to have acted professionally, which would have prevented the suicide attempt.

Mary's lawyer will also be developing a narrative of the case. The major themes would likely include the limitations of hindsight analysis. Hindsight can make the unpredictable seem inevitable (Schultz 2000:346). The narrative would stress that mental health providers have a limited ability to predict suicide dangers. Further, a mental health provider sees a client for only a limited amount of time and thus has little opportunity to control the behavior of an outpatient client, particularly one whose treatment had ended. Finally, the lawyer would develop the question of whether it is appropriate to compel a social worker in private practice to continue to treat a threatening client with a violent history. The lawyer might ask the jurors to consider whether they would continue to work with someone who had threatened them at their work site. The message that the lawyer would seek to convey is that Mary met professional standards when she referred Cora to her psychiatrist. Cora's subsequent suicide attempt was an exercise of free will, beyond the control or influence of Mary.

PRODUCTION OF EVIDENCE. The opening statements establish the themes and present a rationale and structure for each side to prove its theory of the case. The plaintiff or prosecutor is first to present evidence. In most situations the plaintiff/prosecutor has the burden of proving the essential elements of the legal claim. This means that the plaintiff/prosecutor must produce direct testimony and/or physical evidence and carefully choreograph the introduction of each piece to address every issue and to anticipate every defense. In a few situations the burden of proof shifts to the defendant once the essential facts have been established. For example, in employment discrimination cases, where the employer has control of most sources of evidence, the plaintiff has the initial burden of proving the basic facts that could support a complaint of discrimination. Then the burden shifts to the defendant company to prove the existence of nondiscriminatory reasons for terminating the employee (*Texas Department of Community Affairs v. Burdine* [1981]).

RULES OF EVIDENCE. The collection and presentation of evidence in court are governed by legal rules designed to prevent fraudulent testimony, to exclude faulty or misleading evidence, and to protect constitutional rights. A second reason for a court to construct rules concerning the admissibility of evidence is that a court restricts its scrutiny to the facts that are material to the legal issues of the case and relevant to proving or disproving the facts (*Black's* 1983). Evidence is the essential nutrient for a developing case. Evidence may be in the form of oral testimony by a witness or physical evidence offered as proof of an alleged fact. As we have seen, during the pretrial process judges place restrictions on the areas to be litigated, which limits the scope of evidence produced for trial.

When the opposing side challenges evidence, the judge must determine whether it is material and relevant. In the case of *Cora v. Mary* evidence of Mary's recent attendance at a seminar on psychotherapy with borderline clients would be material to the case, because her lawyer could use it to refute the contention that she was not prepared to treat people with this diagnosis. However, supportive testimony from another client of Mary's who has a borderline personality disorder would probably not be deemed relevant to proving or disproving the propriety of Mary's treatment of Cora.

Judges may exclude or limit evidence on a variety of other grounds. The most common limitation is on hearsay evidence. Essentially, hearsay evidence is secondhand information. If a witness offers a statement of another person as proof of the truth of an issue, judges generally disallow it (Feinman 2000). For example, the lawyer for Cora's family might try to subpoena Mary's best friend as a witness, to ask her whether Mary ever talked about feeling incompetent to handle Cora's problems. Because the purpose of this testimony would be to prove that Mary knew that she was in over her head but did not seek supervision or consultation, the judge would probably exclude the evidence as hearsay. The hearsay rule has a number of exceptions, but these are beyond the scope of this book.

In some cases a judge excludes evidence that would be useful to arriving at the truth (Feinman 2000). Some evidence, usually information about a past event, is considered so prejudicial that a jury making a judgment about the present case never learns of it. Suppose Cora once was arrested for physically assaulting her therapist at a juvenile correctional facility. While the evidence might support the validity of Mary's fears, this evidence could predispose the jury to believe that Cora would have followed through on her threats and that Mary was justified in terminating treatment. The judge probably would exclude this type of evidence because of its prejudicial effect on the jury.

Finally, judges exclude some evidence on public policy grounds. Evidence law protects certain relationships in society. While the general rule is to admit all material and relevant evidence and to obtain the testimony of every person who has such evidence, statutes and case law define some communications as protected by testimonial privilege. Doctor-patient, lawyer-client, priest-penitent, psychotherapist-client, and spousal privilege are common forms found in most jurisdictions. In these examples maintaining confidentiality is vital to support open communications essential to these relationships. Finally, constitutional privilege protects individuals from being compelled to give self-incriminating evidence concerning a criminal matter.

Evidence law requires authentication of physical evidence before it is introduced officially as evidence. The attorney does this by calling a witness to the stand who can identify the item and testify to its authenticity and relevance to the case. Once this is done, the lawyer may ask the judge to accept the numbered exhibit as evidence. The opposing counsel may object on grounds of relevance, materiality, prejudicial effects, or other reasons. Returning to our case, in Mary's direct testimony her attorney may ask her to identify Cora's case record and stipulate that it is complete and accurate. The attorney would then need to have the judge accept it before eliciting testimony about the case record.

TESTIMONY OF A FACT WITNESS. Witnesses who have some firsthand knowledge of the events or issues in a case are sometimes called fact witnesses to differentiate them from expert witnesses (discussed shortly). The lawyer directs the fact witness to attend court by having the person served with a subpoena that details the time and place to appear. The lawyer then calls the fact witness to the stand and conducts the direct examination. A direct examination has several goals. First, the lawyer asks demographic (foundation) questions to establish the identification of the witness and his or her relationship to the case. The lawyer should carefully plan the questions in direct examination to guide the witness's telling of the story and to emphasize the information that supports the lawyer's theory of the case. The questioning should allow the judge and jury to follow the story in a logical and chronological sequence. An experienced lawyer uses simple terminology and reorients the jury when interruptions to the flow of testimony occur, such as objections, the introduction of physical evidence, or when a court recesses for lunch (Crump and Berman 1985).

Social workers called to testify as fact witnesses need to understand the questioning process. A social work witness should be prepared to answer the foundation questions with specific information such as level of education, dates of graduation, and the length of time employed in one's current job. Because the questions on direct examination tend to be closed, social workers should limit their responses to the specific issue that the lawyer has asked about. Lawyers are not allowed to ask leading questions on direct examination (Kaplan and Waltz 1987). These are questions that suggest the expected answer, such as, "You were afraid of Cora, weren't you?"

It is important that witnesses testify only about information for which they have direct knowledge. For example, a witness should describe observed behaviors (he was stumbling and unsteady) and other indications of alcohol consumption (strong smell of liquor) rather than stating a conclusion that the man was drunk. Social workers who are directed to bring a copy of their clinical notes to court need to review the laws of the state governing privileged communication and the status of psychotherapy notes. A judge generally allows a witness to refer to notes to refresh her or his memory on issues such as the number of sessions held or the date of an intake.

Following the direct examination, the defense is allowed to cross-examine the witness. The goal of cross-examination is to bring out inconsistencies, weakness, and errors in the direct testimony. Because of this the style of questioning is substantively different from direct testimony. In some cases the cross examination is hostile or aggressive, and the lawyer who is cross-examining the witness uses leading questions to try to push the witness into a statement that reduces the veracity and credibility of the direct testimony or impeaches the character and qualifications of the witness.

Some questions may be intentionally ambiguous or complex in order to provoke a confused or unprofessional response. Lawyers may seek to question a witness's perception or memory and therefore the witness's ability to describe the events accurately. Further, questions might attempt to uncover a bias or a monetary interest in the case (Kaplan and Waltz 1987). The social work witness who focuses on the purpose of the cross-examination will find it is easier to refrain from personalizing the attacks. Witnesses often find it useful to pause before answering a question posed by the attorney conducting the cross-examination. This allows time for opposing counsel to raise an objection and gives the witness an opportunity to consider the form and intent of the question.

TESTIMONY OF AN EXPERT WITNESS. Many legal disputes involve technical or specialized subjects that are beyond the knowledge and experience of ordinary jurors. Did the design of a product conform to generally accepted engineering standards for the industry? What is the significance of finding a blade of a particular type of grass in the car of a murder defendant? What constitutes effective psychotherapy treatment for people with a borderline personality disorder? Expert witnesses, who have specialized knowledge in the subject area, provide opinions and interpret information for the jury, in direct contrast to ordinary witnesses, who must limit testimony to their direct knowledge of the facts of the case (Kaplan and Waltz 1987).

The lawyers use information provided by expert witnesses to establish the context for evaluating the actions of the parties in the lawsuit or criminal case

(Barker and Branson 2000). As with other types of evidence, the other side frequently challenges the testimony and exhibits of an expert witness before a judge decides to allow, reject, or limit the testimony. A judge may ask the lawyer to make an offer of proof (i.e., whether the testimony has probative value for any element of the legal case) before ruling on the admissibility of the testimony. In addition, a lawyer may challenge expert testimony on the basis of its scientific integrity.

The testimony of expert witnesses is influential to the determination of guilt or liability by the jury. Judges are cautious in admitting testimony about unproved theories, or what has been pejoratively referred to as junk science. The most notorious example may have been the so-called Twinkie defense in which an expert testified that the criminal defendant's junk food diet was part of the symptomatology of clinical depression, which led to an inability to control his impulses. This case involved the killing of the mayor of San Francisco by Dan White. The jury found White guilty but agreed with the expert's testimony concerning his diminished capacity. It failed to find White guilty on the murder charge, opting instead for the less serious charge of voluntary manslaughter (Mounts 1999).

The U.S. Supreme Court, in a 1993 case popularly known as *Daubert*, established four criteria that scientific evidence must meet to be admissible in the federal courts (most states use similar standards). The standard includes whether the theory or technique has been tested or can be tested, has been subjected to a peer review processes, has a known error rate, and is generally accepted within the relevant professional community (*Daubert v. Merrell Dow Pharmaceuticals* [1993]). Thus under the *Daubert* standard for scientific testimony to be admitted, it must first be determined to be reliable, material, and based on scientifically valid reasoning and methodology (Spadaro 1998).

The *Daubert* standard focuses on scientific evidence, which has created controversy in some jurisdictions about to how to treat social science evidence. Some courts apply a more lenient test, giving judges broad discretion to decide on the admissibility of expert testimony (Zirogiannis 2001). The rules for admitting expert evidence from the social sciences are not clear beyond the need for the judge to fulfill a gatekeeping role to keep out evidence that is unreliable or prejudicial (*Kumho Tire v. Carmichael* [1999]). For example, a social worker may be asked to serve as an expert witness in a custody case. A father may be claiming that his child's mother is unduly influencing the child to repeat angry statements, including making up stories of sexual abuse. The social worker's expert testimony about "parental alienation syndrome" (the theory that one parent brainwashes a child to adopt negative views and reject the other parent) could support the father's case (Faller 1998). A judge would have to decide whether the research about this syndrome is sufficiently reliable to allow the expert testimony.

Let us imagine that the lawyer for Cora's family finds a psychiatrist who is willing to testify that psychotherapy is completely ineffective with clients who have personality disorders and that the only effective treatment is behavior modification. Further, he is willing to testify that psychotherapy is dangerous for this population because it often results in clients' harming themselves. Mary's lawyer hires a local professor of clinical psychology who is willing to testify that the cognitive-behavioral therapy that Mary used is an empirically sound treatment approach. The judge would hold a hearing to assess the scientific integrity of each witness's evidence before deciding whether either or both are admissible.

Social workers are sometimes asked to serve as expert witnesses. An expert social worker can provide the best answer to the question of whether a social worker has violated a social work ethics or practice standard. In addition, social workers are frequently recognized as experts in child abuse, family issues such as custody or guardianship, and mental health diagnosis and treatment. An expert often has not seen the client but testifies about clinical or practice issues and then may be asked to give an opinion related to the case, given the evidence and facts.

In some cases social workers testifying as fact witnesses are asked to serve as experts. A lawyer may ask the judge to certify a social worker as an expert in order to ask for opinion testimony. Social workers should avoid this dual role in a proceeding because it carries ethical and practice dilemmas. Expert testimony is supposed to be objective, based on the specialized knowledge of the witness. Treating clinicians may be asked to give opinions that would be against the interests of their clients, potentially violating a social worker's ethical responsibility to give priority to the interests of the client (NASW 1999). Giving testimony that is contrary to the interests of one's client violates the fiduciary nature of a therapeutic relationship. Further, it complicates future treatment by introducing a role that may conflict with the therapeutic alliance (Strasburger, Gutheil, and Brodsky 1997).

Lawyers and judges who do not understand social work practice and ethical guidelines may try to force practitioners to serve as expert witnesses. This is likely to occur in cases where little money is available to pay for an expert and where the issues involve decisions about a client's family or mental health.

In these cases judges must make decisions, yet they often have no professional training to understand the dynamics of human behavior. They are looking for information and expert opinion to help them to make complex, Solomon-like decisions. One way to reduce inappropriate judicial requests is to ensure that direct testimony is complete, professional, and helpful to the court. When social work testimony is vague and no other source of guidance is available, legal professionals are more likely to look around the court for someone to help them reach a safe and appropriate resolution to the case.

At the close of the plaintiff's case the defendant may make a motion for a dismissal of the case, often called a directed verdict. In this motion the defendant argues that the evidence offered as proof by the plaintiff or prosecutor is insufficient to prove the necessary elements of the legal claim. If the judge does not grant this motion, the trial continues, with the defendant offering evidence to disprove the plaintiff's case. At the close of their case defendants may again petition the judge to grant a dismissal.

CLOSING STATEMENTS. The plaintiff or prosecutor presents a closing argument, followed by the defense. The closing argument reviews and highlights the most favorable evidence. One task for the attorney is to develop a narrative linking the various pieces of evidence together and highlighting the themes of the case while minimizing adverse evidence.

JURY INSTRUCTIONS. In jury trials the lawyers for each side submit to the judge proposed instructions for the jury. The judge determines the language that represents the substantive law on which the jury must decide the case. The judge ordinarily reads the instructions to the jury and provides guidelines for jurors to follow in coming to a decision. In some cases the judge issues a series of specific questions for the jury to answer in its deliberations.

DELIBERATIONS AND JUDGMENT. The first task of a jury is to elect a foreperson, who presides over the deliberations. A jury's decision must be unanimous in civil cases in most states, although some states require a majority, such as nine out of twelve jurors' finding for one side. In criminal cases the verdict must be unanimous. As previously discussed, the standard of proof in a civil case is different than in a criminal case. If the jurors reach an impasse, the judge may ask them to reconsider the evidence and eventually may declare a mistrial. In these cases the parties have the right to present the case for a new trial. If the jury reaches a verdict, the foreperson presents the verdict to the court.

REMEDIES AND PENALTIES. Judges, public officials, and law enforcement personnel have the authority to enforce the decisions of the court regarding compensation and/or punishment (Winfield 1995). Without this power the decisions of courts would be empty and social order would be sacrificed.

When a civil suit is successful, the court has the responsibility to enforce the verdict through an appropriate remedy. The most familiar form of remedy involves monetary damages. Courts may award monetary compensation to the plaintiff for injuries and damages suffered as a result of the defendant's conduct. The damage award is based on direct compensation for losses or it may be calculated based on the amount that it would take to restore the plaintiffs to their status or position before the action of the defendant. Judges are allowed to consider claims for punitive damages in some types of civil cases.

Although punitive damages are awarded infrequently, they are controversial part of the U.S. judicial system. The three policy reasons for imposing punitive damages are deterrence, retribution, and compensation (Klinck 2001). In some cases the only way to deter continued negligent or harmful acts by an individual or industry is to make continuing the acts too expensive. Other times, the behavior of the defendant was wanton, willful, or malicious, or the injury was so catastrophic or horrific that a higher level of damages is justified.

In some legal controversies a judge might issue a court order requiring a defendant to perform some act or refrain from doing something. This type of remedy is called equitable relief. In these cases the judge rules on the facts. For example, recall the case example of the managed-care lawsuit. If the consumers prevail in that case, the court's remedy might be in the form of another court order, requiring the managed-care company to drop its proposed coverage changes.

In criminal cases and other noncriminal violations of the law, judges may decide on the appropriate penalty. Some statutes are specific about the penalty, whereas others allow judges to select the penalty from an approved range. The so-called three strikes laws, for example, limit the discretion of federal court judges in the sentencing of people convicted of a third serious violent crime or drug offense (see the Violent Crime Control and Law Enforcement Act of 1994). When a judge has discretion, social workers are in a position to urge alternative sentencing.

POSTTRIAL MOTIONS AND APPEALS. The losing side may ask the judge to reconsider the decision of a jury. If the judge finds that the jury's decision was not based on the law, the judge may overturn the jury verdict. A losing party may also ask the judge for a new trial based on a judicial mistake made during the trial. If this type of motion is accepted, the court is likely to grant a new trial.

As I outlined in chapter 3, either party can appeal the final decision of a court to a higher court. In some cases an appeal can be taken earlier in a trial. If the judge in *Cora v. Mary* decided that the appropriate venue for the trial was in neighboring state B, it would be unjust to disallow an appeal until a final decision was reached in the trial. The appeal of a crucial issue before or during a trial is called an interlocutory appeal. In some jurisdictions this type of appeal is called a writ, and lawyers use it to ask an appeals court to order a judge to take an action or prevent a judicial action.

The appellate courts generally do not review how the judge or jury in the trial court judged the facts. The limited exception is if the appeals court finds no substantial evidence to support the finding of fact. The primary role of an appeals court is to review questions of law. During the trial lawyers make objections to judicial rulings on the admission or exclusion of evidence, selection of applicable statutes, reading of a law, instructions to the jury, and other similar matters. Either party may appeal a trial court's application of the law to the case.

An appeals court has several options in reviewing a case. It may find that the trial judge committed an error in applying the law and that this had a direct effect on the outcome. In this circumstance the appellate court may throw out the judgment of the trial court and order a new trial. Sometimes the appeals court determines that an error has been made but that the error was harmless. In other words, even if the judge had decided the legal question correctly, the outcome would not have changed. In these cases the appeals court may uphold the trial court's decision. At the appeals stage the issues of law become isolated, and the case may turn on a very technical question. In the various stages of appeal the law is refined. Because of this, appeals courts publish their decisions.

Litigation is a complicated and technical process that governs the way that the legal system applies the law to a set of facts in order to resolve a conflict. The conduct of lawyers must be understood within the context of the legal issues that might emerge as the process unfolds. Social workers focus on the present and are encouraged to engage in creative problem solving. Lawyers are always cognizant of the effect of current actions on the ability to pursue legal options in the future and are counseled to refrain from doing anything that might compromise a legal right or preclude a legal option for a client. Social workers can be effective participants in litigation as advocates, participants, witnesses, or consultants when they understand the purposes and processes of litigation and legal action.

6.

PROTECTION OF INDIVIDUALS AND
THE PRESERVATION OF SOCIAL ORDER

We the People of the United States, in Order to form a more perfect Union,
establish justice, insure domestic Tranquility, provide for the common
defence, promote the general Welfare, and secure the Blessings of Liberty
to ourselves and our Posterity, do ordain and establish this Constitution
for the United States of America. —Preamble, U.S. Constitution

CONSTITUTIONAL PROTECTIONS AND
AMERICAN VALUES

Social workers who understand basic constitutional principles can be more effective in their work on behalf of clients and in interacting with legal systems.
The NASW *Code of Ethics* obligates social workers to engage in social and political action to ensure equal access to societal resources and opportunities
(1999:standard 6.04). Social workers sometimes recognize injustices or unfair
actions by state or federal agencies against clients. Other times, police or prosecutors may use questionable means in pursuing the arrest of a suspect and the
trial of a criminal defendant. Social workers employed by government agencies
develop and implement policies regarding benefits and entitlements. In each
case a working knowledge of constitutional law will improve the social worker's practice.

The equality and civil rights components of the Constitution have been
used to further social policy goals for poor and oppressed populations, especially by the Warren Court. Although the current majority of justices have retreated from the activist approach of earlier iterations of the Supreme Court,
constitutional law is likely to continue to advance social policy. The historic
Supreme Court decisions, affirming civil and other human rights and protecting people from discrimination, are the threads of the fabric of the entire legal
system. As such, judicial decisions in every court in the nation reflect the fundamental principles of constitutional law.

The Constitution is an astoundingly brief yet complex statement of the principles of American freedom and the relationships among individuals, states,

and the federal government. It consists of seven articles that describe the structure of the federal government, the duties of each branch, and the procedures for the election and appointment of government officials. The Constitution has been amended twenty-seven times since its ratification, including the set of amendments generally referred to as the Bill of Rights. The Bill of Rights sets out the principles of equality and individual liberty and thus is the most relevant part of the Constitution for social workers to understand.

Because the Constitution is the ultimate legal standard, no laws or government actions can violate these principles. In daily practice lawyers assess the implications of constitutional rights for the actions of the government. Did the action follow due process? Did it violate fundamental rights or freedoms? Did a regulation or a statute give adequate notice proscribing a particular course of action? In popular discourse people commonly refer to constitutional rights as societal values. "I can say what I want to say, it's freedom of speech!" Indeed, constitutional rights have taken on a broader cultural significance than their legal reality. The Constitution protects citizens from the actions of the government, and generally, it is the government and its agents, through laws, regulations, or other actions, that violate an individual's constitutional rights. Knowledge of constitutional rights enables lawyers and social workers to provide a high level of advocacy to clients.

The Constitution affects the rights of people in society through both assurances and restrictions. The Constitution specifies a range of liberties that individuals enjoy. Establishing limitations on the powers of government secures the rights of individuals. This is consistent with the philosophical stance of the early leaders of the American government, who distrusted powerful government authority.

The development of constitutional thought occurs through the common law process, with a series of cases interpreting various constitutional principles. The Constitution is written in general language, allowing scholars and ordinary citizens to argue about the scope and meaning of virtually every word of the document. For example, does the Second Amendment's promise of the right to bear arms protect gun ownership today, or is it reflective of the era in which it was written, when citizen militias were a necessary part of national defense? It is important to consider whether arguments about the Constitution are based on legitimate philosophical disagreements, diverse moral positions, convenient political positions, or some combination of all these factors.

The core issues in constitutional law involve interpretation of the language of the document. Often, the argument sounds like this: the originalists, or strict constructionists, argue that the framers of the Constitution set up a near-ly perfect document. We should look to the original language or intent to determine how to apply a constitutional principle to a current legal controversy, and we should refrain from developing new areas of constitutional law. The originalists believe that the place to create new law is the legislature, where the democratic process can operate to reflect the will of the people.

The opposing argument, developed by those sometimes referred to as nonoriginalists, insists that the provisions of the Constitution are necessarily vague in order to be flexible to respond to new circumstances and changing societal needs. In this view the interpretation of the Constitution should reflect the beliefs and morals of contemporary society. An important component of this approach is to allow the courts to extend constitutional principles to protect the rights of less powerful individuals and groups whose rights may not be respected by a majority political process. The judicial activism and protection of less powerful segments of the population supported by this view of constitutional interpretation are consistent with the advocacy stance of the social work profession. Lofty academic aspects of the Constitution are worth advanced study by social workers. However, knowledge of a few essential constitutional rights and protections is critical to social workers who are promoting social justice, defending individual rights, and working effectively with lawyers.

The key values served by the Constitution are liberty and equality. These values take several forms, but focusing on these first principles helps to keep the material from becoming too abstract and inaccessible. Liberty has several dimensions that correspond to guarantees of individual rights and freedoms. The protections in the Bill of Rights enable citizens to be free of unnecessary government intrusions and preserve the rights of citizens to criticize their government or take unpopular stances. Due process protects individuals from arbitrary actions by the government to deprive them of life, liberty, or property. Other civil rights, such as the right to vote and the right to assemble, ensure that individuals have the freedom to participate in the decisions of government.

Equality is the second primary constitutional value that supports social justice. Equal protection under the law is the constitutional principle that gives life to this value. A logical extension of equal protection is to assume that if everyone is equal, each person should be treated in the same way and the government should not allow discriminatory laws or practices that limit the opportunities of any group. However, in order to reverse discriminatory practices that have existed in society, the government may be allowed to create laws in which certain groups are treated differently, albeit to their advantage.

In some circumstances adherence to these first principles may conflict. In order to enhance equality we may have to limit liberty, as is the case with the Americans with Disabilities Act and affirmative action policies. The United States celebrates the collective action of democracy, but the power of the people to decide public policy in a democratic way is subject to some limitations. Some individual rights are so fundamental that they must be protected even if the majority wish otherwise (Kennedy 1990). For example, supporting liberty may require the government to protect the odious speech of a hate group because to do otherwise would threaten the foundation of free speech. Because democratic practices may not result in the support of each individual's constitutional rights, we rely on judicial review to protect against government abuse of power. The genius of the framers of the Constitution was that they avoided writing a blueprint for society yet set up a system that recognizes private rights (Kennedy 1990). The courts' job is to act as a referee when individual actions and government powers conflict.

INDIVIDUAL LIBERTY AND CIVIL RIGHTS

The Bill of Rights protects individuals from interference by the government. These liberties include freedom of speech, freedom of the press, the right of citizens to assemble, freedom of religion, and the right to vote, among others. The initial ten amendments that make up the Bill of Rights were passed in 1791 following ratification of the document by the states in order to limit the powers of the federal government. After the Civil War Americans approved the Fourteenth Amendment, which prohibits states from abridging the rights and immunities of any citizen without due process of law. The Supreme Court has interpreted this clause as extending to the states the constitutional limitations on the power of the government to restrict individual liberties.

Due process rights are the fulfillment of the first principle of liberty. Generically, the Constitution, through the Fifth and Fourteenth Amendments, grants citizens the right not to be deprived of life, liberty, or property without due process. Due process analysis has two levels. One is the essential guarantee of procedural process that is provided to an individual. Before a government entity can act to restrict life, liberty, or property, it must provide the person with adequate notice and a right to be heard in an official proceeding. Often the determination of whether a government action has deprived a person of a right or merely a government privilege determines whether any process is due.

The second type of due process is substantive due process. The question in a substantive due process analysis is whether the government was justified in denying or restricting the life, liberty, or property of a person.

PROCEDURAL DUE PROCESS AND ADMINISTRATIVE LAW

Procedural due process guarantees have created a series of cases that have served to standardize the procedures that administrative agencies use. Because administrative agencies are charged with distributing social services and public benefits, social workers need knowledge of the extent of due process. In *Goldberg v. Kelly* (1970) the Supreme Court found that states must hold hearings for welfare recipients before states can terminate benefits. In order to reach this conclusion, the Court found the benefits to be a protectable interest under the Constitution because of the recipients' reliance on these benefits for survival (i.e., a property right). In the case of welfare benefits, school suspensions (*Goss v. Lopez* [1975]), and other significant denials of government benefits, the government has to provide a minimal level of process, usually including a chance for the recipient to be heard and an opportunity for a review of the decision to terminate or deny benefits. However, not every denial of a benefit triggers a requirement for a hearing, and courts often find that any process is sufficient process.

Some basic elements of procedural due process include adequate and timely notice, the right be heard, the right to have the decision made a matter of record, and the right to appeal the decision. Depending on the setting, the individual may also have the right to be represented by an attorney and the right to cross-examine witnesses. The key issue is whether the government acted in an arbitrary manner to deny a protected right to an individual.

Due process procedures form the backbone of administrative law. Agencies generally use the level of process that is consistent with the type of interest at stake. For example, state agencies that license social workers have extensive formal procedures in place that an agency must follow before it can revoke a license to practice. A fundamental principle of administrative law is that a person must exhaust all available administrative processes before filing a complaint in court. Social workers acting as advocates should document each level of administrative review in order to avoid the delay and expense of a court's rejecting a complaint on the ground that all levels of administrative review have not been completed.

SUBSTANTIVE DUE PROCESS AND FUNDAMENTAL RIGHTS

Substantive due process is the second type of due process review. Once again the threshold question is whether the government may act to deny a protected interest in life, liberty, or property. Cases in this area arise from challenges to statutes, regulations, or government actions regarding a class or group of citizens. The key issue is whether the right is a *fundamental* liberty or property right. A law can deprive a person of a basic liberty or property right so long as the statute is rationally related to a legitimate state interest. The 1986 case of *Bowers v. Hardwick* illustrates this point. In *Bowers* a man challenged a Georgia statute that criminalized sodomy. The Supreme Court found that the right to engage in consensual sexual activity is not a fundamental liberty. Georgia needed to show only that its ban was rationally related to its interest in proscribing homosexual activity. Courts generally will not question the legislative judgment or the legitimacy of the statute, so there is little meaningful review of cases when no fundamental rights are involved.

If court determines that a right is fundamental, the scrutiny of the statute is much more stringent. The state's objective in enacting the statute must be compelling, and the statute must be narrowly drawn to further the compelling state interest (Vandevelde 1998). The standard of review is called strict scrutiny. When the court finds that a statute infringes on a fundamental liberty, it usually invalidates the statute.

In *Zablocki v. Redhail* (1978) the statute in question was a policy that denied a marriage license to noncustodial parents who owed child support. The Supreme Court found that the right to marry is a fundamental liberty. It examined the state's interest in ensuring that all parents support their biological children, even when they remarry. The Court invalidated the law because it was not narrowly drawn and was not likely to further the state's interest. The policy of withholding marriage licenses may have resulted in fewer couples applying for legal marriages instead of ensuring that applicants cleared all their all outstanding child support debts.

The constitutional analysis of what constitutes a fundamental right has been the conclusive issue in most of these cases. Because the Constitution does not list every interest that creates a fundamental right, the Court has struggled to find a consistent standard for review. Does the fundamental right to liberty include the autonomy to make decisions involving personal and family or child-rearing decisions? The Supreme Court, in a series of decisions, has found that these areas (including abortion, parenting, and access to birth control but not consensual homosexual activity) are within the broad but undefined right of privacy. Therefore, any statutes or regulations that restrict individual privacy rights face a difficult constitutional challenge under the doctrine of substantive due process.

However, the Supreme Court is reluctant to extend substantive due process protections in new areas. For example, in the well-known child welfare case of *DeShaney v. Winnebago County Department of Social Services* (1989), the Court rejected the assertion that the state's failure to protect a child from an abusive father constituted a constitutional violation. Despite extensive evidence of maltreatment and that state workers were aware of it, the Court reasoned that the harm was created by the actions of a private individual, the father. In part, the Court was reluctant to find a right in this case lest it create an affirmative duty for the states to protect individuals from harm in a variety of cases. If police were informed of a threat, or a school employee heard about a planned fight, would they have a constitutional duty to prevent the harm? The Court was unwilling to extend substantive due process rights despite enormous sympathy for the child in *DeShaney*. The justices' repeated laments during oral arguments of "poor Joshua" did not overcome the principle, and the unfortunate result, in this case.

THE EQUAL PROTECTION DOCTRINE

To the untrained eye there would seem to be few differences in the way that the due process and equal protection clauses operate to limit the power of the government. That is because the standards for analysis are nearly identical, and the courts have used both doctrines to justify decisions over time. The key difference is that equal protection should be used when the harm accrues to a particular group rather than to an individual. Equal protection under the law is about limiting the government's ability to discriminate against classes of people.

All laws classify citizens in one manner or another. Some states require youth who are learning to drive to have an adult in the car with them during a probationary period. Other laws prohibit youth younger than eighteen from driving late at night. Elderly drivers are required to renew their licenses and to pass vision tests more frequently than other drivers. Welfare benefits and financial aid for college may be awarded only to those who meet income guidelines. These laws each discriminate against a class of people, yet they do not violate the equal protection clause. Inclusions or exclusions in a rule or a program usually are intended to further the goals of the legislation.

When a statute makes a classification that has a rational relationship to a legitimate state purpose, courts generally reject equal protection claims and uphold the law. When a statute involves a fundamental right, or when the statute makes a suspect classification based on race or national origin, a court will examine whether the intention was to discriminate, whether the law serves a compelling state interest, and whether the classification is necessary to achieve the purpose of the statute. When the statute classification has involved gender or other suspect classifications, the courts have held states to a heightened scrutiny. A recent example of a statute that violated the equal protection clause involved sexual orientation.

After various Colorado municipalities passed ordinances banning discrimination based on sexual orientation, Colorado voters adopted an amendment to the state constitution. The amendment precluded legislative, executive, or judicial action at any level of state or local government that was designed to protect the status of people based on their homosexual, lesbian, or bisexual orientation, conduct, practices, or relationships. A group of citizens challenged the statute under the equal protection doctrine. The state's principal argument was that the amendment puts gays and lesbians in the same position as all other people by denying them special rights. The amendment's immediate effects were to repeal all existing statutes, regulations, ordinances, and policies of state and local entities that barred discrimination based on sexual orientation and to prohibit any government entity from adopting similar, or more protective, measures in the future.

The Supreme Court agreed to review the case and found that this disqualification of a class of people from the right to obtain specific protection from the law was unprecedented and was itself a denial of equal protection in the most literal sense. Second, the justices found the sheer breadth of the amendment was so far removed from the reasons offered for it (i.e., respect for other citizens' freedom of association and the state's interest in conserving resources to fight discrimination against other groups), that the amendment "cannot be explained by reference to those reasons" (*Romer v. Evans*, 517 U.S. 620, 634 [1996]). The Court found that the amendment raised "the inevitable inference that it is born of animosity toward the class that it affects" and is not directed to an "identifiable legitimate purpose or discrete objective" (634, 635). The Court concluded by finding that the amendment was a status-based classification of people undertaken for its own sake, something that the equal protection clause does not permit (635).

Equal protection and due process cases tend to be complex and full of arcane analysis. In practice these constitutional limits on government authority are most helpful at a higher level of abstraction. Has someone been treated fairly by a law or a public agency? Is a decision arbitrary or discriminatory? Has the government followed its procedures and allowed for appeals? Does a law have a disproportionately negative effect on a group or does it seem to deny an individual a fundamental right? This is the type of thinking that lawyers use as they represent their clients. Social workers who recognize questionable practices and regulations can empower clients to demand their rights, alert civil rights advocates to the need for action, and speak with a more authoritative voice in legal settings.

The material on civil rights discussed earlier suggests that the only way to remedy an alleged violation is to try to challenge the statute or law. Congress has enacted several laws that allow people to sue or to initiate criminal complaints to enforce civil rights laws. The most significant statute, 42 U.S.C. 1983 (2001) (popularly known as section 1983), allows a private suit for damages to be brought against anyone who "under the color of any statute" deprives the person of any "rights, privileges or immunities secured by the Constitution and laws." This law allows those who have been mistreated by police or other government officials to challenge those acts in court. Other federal statutes provide legal recourse when a person has been deprived of a federally guaranteed right; one allows an individual to sue a private (nongovernment) person or a group of people who conspire to deprive someone of a civil right (48 U.S.C. 1985[c] [2001]).

CRIMINAL LAW AND CRIMINAL PROCEDURE

A crime is a violation of a statute that criminalizes a particular behavior. The requirement that a criminal statute be specific about the particular behavior outlawed arises from the constitutional requirement of notice. Each criminal statute specifies the elements of a crime, including the act or conspiracy to act, the circumstances under which the act occurs (with a gun, against a minor), and the state of mind or intent (knowingly, with recklessness, purposefully). A prosecutor must prove each element of a crime beyond a reasonable doubt in order to convict a defendant of a crime.

The actions of individuals who violate criminal statues compromise the liberty interests of individuals who make up a community. Therefore, the government has a duty to pursue criminal prosecutions to protect life, liberty, and property (Stith 1993). The government's concern about law enforcement must be balanced against the limits on police power and the rights of the accused that are articulated in the Constitution. The overriding purpose of constitutional protections is to restrict the government from pursuing its interests at the expense of an individual's autonomy and privacy. Yet the government, through its legal systems, courts, and public defenders, is charged with upholding the protection of these individual rights.

This can be a difficult balance to strike. When does the constitutional principle take precedence over the pursuit of the truth or of justice? Why should society accept the use of a technicality to free a person who is widely assumed to be guilty of a crime? Why do lawyers want to defend people who are often guilty of many offenses? The reasons are complex, but not least among these is that protection of individual rights and enforcing limitations on the power of the government to control citizens and to silence opposition is crucial to maintaining the first principles of liberty and equality.

The Bill of Rights contains several of the most important rights in the criminal context. The Fourth Amendment limits the power of the government to invade the privacy of individuals by granting the "right of the people to be secure in their persons, houses, papers, and effects, against unreasonable searches and seizures." The police must demonstrate probable cause and request a search of a specific place or person in order for a judge to issue a search warrant. If the search or seizure of evidence is found to be improper, a judge may exclude its use at trial, even if it means allowing a guilty defendant to go free. Here again protecting the principle is more important than winning an individual case.

The Fifth Amendment contains a number of criminal protections. It requires a grand jury indictment before the state can charge a person with a serious crime. It also prohibits trying someone twice for the same offense (double jeopardy) and confers the right against self-incrimination (this is the source of the expression "to plead the Fifth"). The Sixth Amendment provides the right to a speedy and public trial by an impartial jury. The right to counsel and the right to confront witnesses during a criminal trial are among the Sixth Amendment protections. The jury selection process protects a criminal defendant's due process rights. Either the defense attorney or the prosecutor may exclude a prospective juror during voir dire if either has a concern about bias or partiality. Some cases have defined an "impartial jury" as one drawn from a panel that accurately reflects that community and is selected with nondiscriminatory criteria (Eisemann 2001). However, prosecuting and defense attorneys continue to pursue a strategy of racial and gender stacking of juries.

Those trained in the law view the duty to preserve a criminal defendant's rights as sacrosanct. This duty to the legal system and its fundamental principles, combined with the duty of zealous representation, results in aggressive (some might say obnoxious) criminal defense lawyers. Social workers need to develop an appreciation of the importance of the rights of criminal defendants and the job of the defense lawyer in order to establish strong working relationships with defense lawyers in criminal contexts.

SPECIAL TREATMENT OF JUVENILE CRIMINAL OFFENSES

Minor children have few legal rights. Historically, juveniles who committed crimes were tried in adult courts and given sentences in adult prisons. During the Progressive Era social reformers pressed for the courts to treat youthful offenders differently in recognition of youngsters' need for nurturing and guidance rather than punishment (Justice Policy Institute 1999). These reformers fought for the establishment of specialized juvenile courts, including the creation of juvenile detention facilities to serve youth who needed to be incarcerated (Jansson 1997).

The role of juvenile court judges was to act in place of a parent (the *parens patriae* doctrine) for those minor children who committed a delinquent act. As the juvenile court system developed, the emphasis was on treatment and rehabilitation rather than punishment and retribution (Spon 1998). The original juvenile courts provided some procedural safeguards, but youth were not afforded the same constitutional rights as adult defendants (Juvenile Court Act of 1899). In the 1960s juvenile courts began to place a greater emphasis on the criminal nature of juvenile offenses, which led to increases in incarceration (Scott and Grisso 1997). These stiffer penalties raised constitutional concerns about improper denial of the liberty rights and eventually were challenged in the Supreme Court case *In re* Gault (1967). The *Gault* decision granted juveniles more procedural due process rights, including the right to notice of charges, right to an attorney, right to confront witnesses, and right to a fair trial.

In effect, the granting of constitutional rights to juveniles reduced the flexibility of the courts to meet the best interests of the youth. The juvenile court system became increasingly adversarial and formal as the focus turned toward punishment and confinement of juvenile offenders. In the 1990s juvenile courts and prosecutors in most states were given the discretion to transfer tri-

als of serious crimes to adult criminal court, which could sentence guilty defendants to adult prisons for extended periods, rather than release them when
they turned eighteen and the juvenile court's authority ended.

Recently, reforms have sought to implement best practices for juvenile
courts based on outcome research. These initiatives include diversion programs, mediation and restitution programs, specialized probation programs,
and community reintegration programs to assist juveniles returning to the
community after a court-ordered placement or confinement (Kurlychek, Torbet, and Bozynski, 1999). Juvenile courts seem to be approaching a balance between formalized procedures designed to protect the rights of youthful offenders and creative approaches to providing rehabilitative and therapeutic
services to the youth. However, the political pressure to treat serious or violent
offenses in adult courts is unlikely to change.

INFLUENCING LEGAL POLICY

The social work profession must view the law as an institution that is part of
the democratic process of governing. The system can be manipulated to meet
the needs of clients (Madden 2000a). Knowledge of the Constitution and various forms of legal protections gives the social worker access to the primary
tools for influencing legal policy. Social workers should be using legal advocacy to advance civil rights and social justice for individuals and groups that are
underrepresented in the political process. Social workers can do this by calling
attention to patterns of discrimination and brokering legal representation for
clients. Social workers can support legal actions to help individual clients and
disaffected populations through class-action lawsuits. Social workers should be
active in using the legislative process to propose new laws and to change existing laws that violate the rights of clients.

Constitutional cases have resulted in dramatic changes in the manner in
which society responds to its least powerful members. The legislative process
responds most directly to money, power, and influence, the very things denied
to many social work clients. When the political process cannot be swayed,
court challenges are an indispensable strategy. The system of laws relies on
constitutional law as the ultimate arbiter of difficult political and moral problems. Where injustice arises from the ignorance, fervor, or insensitivity of the
legislative or administrative processes, social workers must be able to recognize
the possibilities for legal advocacy in the courts.

7.

HOW COURTS MAKE LEGAL DECISIONS
ABOUT PEOPLE'S LIVES

Family quarrels are bitter things. They don't go according to any rules.
They're not like aches or wounds; they're more like splits in the skin that
won't heal because there's not enough material. —F. Scott Fitzgerald

BALANCING LEGAL RIGHTS AND SOCIAL NEEDS

The greatest challenge for our legal system is to identify standards and procedures for making decisions about peoples' lives. In other parts of the law statutes spell out the elements of a case that, if proved, specify a legal outcome. If a social worker submits a knowingly false insurance claim, saying that he saw a client for ten sessions but actually saw the client only twice, the state may be able to prove a case of fraud. The law provides some discretion for a judge and prosecutor, depending on the circumstances, but the elements of the crime are explicit. No similar formulaic system guides a judge who is asked to decide whether a child should be returned to a home where a parent has a long history of drug abuse and child neglect. Should the grandson of a wealthy elderly woman be granted a general power of attorney? Is it proper for a father who is the custodial parent of a three-year-old to move to another state to take a new job if it would result in the biological mother's not being able to see her child on weekends? How should a domestic violence case be handled?

In cases that deal with life decisions, most courts take the approach of creating rules that balance the interests of people who have legitimate but conflicting interests (American Law Institute 2001). In addition, courts have established procedures to protect those individuals who have limited ability to speak for themselves. In this chapter I will explore some circumstances that give rise to legal decisions that affect the most intimate details of people's lives and the principles that guide legal professionals. The American Law Institute, a think tank, has generated a list of inevitable tensions in family law. These tensions, as adapted here, provide insight into the challenges for legal system as it attempts to make critical life decisions.

The first tension is between legal rules and case-by-case judgments. Because of their training and orientation, legal professionals tend to be most comfortable when they have clearly defined rules. In cases involving peoples' lives, however, individualized decision making is essential. Lawyers can use the same criteria to evaluate every contract, but each family law case generates a unique narrative and set of potential outcomes. Rules must be flexible to respond to the needs of people and circumstances. To effectively manage this challenge lawyers and judges should have a substantial background in family systems theory, developmental theory, and other psychosocial perspectives (S. Brooks 1999). However, it is more realistic to suggest that social workers involved with courts provide insight into these issues for the legal professionals.

Predictability is a fundamental legal value, but it conflicts with the need to respond to each individual situation. The law generally provides people with parameters for behavior that allow lawyers to advise clients about how to comply with the law. Unlike the rigid rules in other areas of the law, family and probate courts have relied on subjective principles, such as the best interests of the child or competency, as the basis for decisions. For one judge a best interest determination may support returning a child to a biological parent. Another judge reviewing the same case could decide that the stability of a grandmother's care is more important. It is little wonder that judges and lawyers turn to social workers and other mental health professionals to provide substantive testimony in these cases. Judges are looking for someone to help them decide the tough cases, to provide an empirical or theoretical basis on which they can rule. Most lawyers want to know that their advocacy position is not putting someone at risk of harm.

As the discussion of the Constitution in chapter 6 suggests, much of our system of law is predicated on distrust of a strong government, and a system of checks on government power. Americans find government intrusion into family life repugnant. Yet they recognize that in some circumstances the protection of individuals or the resolution of conflicts requires judicial intervention. Legal actors may be hesitant to become involved in family life and may demonstrate this reticence in resistance to act, unless the evidence is overwhelming or the risk is substantial.

Individual rights and responsibilities are the foundation of the legal system (S. Brooks 2000). However, family and community systems that are part of the family environment often can be part of the solution. The legal system tends to consider cases from a perspective that asks whose rights should prevail rather than creatively engaging a family to call on its resources to solve its problems. Judges in contested custody disputes often admonish feuding parents not to turn up in court again. Some of these judges discount the reality that the family's circumstances are likely to change in the future, requiring another trip to court. Courts that use more flexible systems of thinking can accommodate developmental changes and evolving family needs. In most courts, if the legal process increases the conflict between parents, each adjustment results in the need for a court to revisit a ruling.

Every day legal professionals in family courts, probate courts, and other judicial settings must practice social work without a license. The legal issues in these cases are best analyzed within a family context, yet the structure of legal representation supports individual advocacy that may not be in the best interest of the client or the family. The knowledge base needed to represent the interests of children, to understand the dynamics of domestic violence, or to assess the competency of an elderly person is beyond the scope and training of most legal professionals. For families to be treated in a therapeutic manner, these cases require substantive participation by social workers, serving as members of interdisciplinary teams in legal settings such as specialized courts, and providing information to the courts as consultants and witnesses. This will occur only when social workers understand the basic principles that guide the decision-making process when family situations require judicial intervention.

THE PROCESS AND ORIENTATION OF FAMILY AND JUVENILE COURTS

The legal processes in family courts are similar to those described in regard to other civil matters. Because each state has its own structure for matters that come before family court, social workers should become familiar with their state's court system. The legal issues most relevant to social workers include divorce, child custody decisions, and child abuse or neglect matters.

Sharon was nineteen and still under the care of the state child welfare department because of a long history of abuse and neglect by her mother. Six months earlier, Sharon had a baby, named Royal, but because she was in a residential program and had no ongoing relationship with Louis, Royal's father, she agreed to allow the child's paternal grandmother to take custody of the baby. Now Sharon has moved into a transition program and is living in a supervised apartment.

She recently learned that Louis, who is twenty-five, has filed a motion with family court to gain custody of his son. Louis's mother has become critically ill and fears that she will not be able to care for Royal. Sharon is committed to gaining custody of Royal and preventing Louis from being involved. Sharon knows that Louis has been in counseling for years, and he has a long history of violent and alcoholic behaviors. Sharon attempted to obtain legal representation from a number of sources without success. Staffers at the primary legal services agency for the poor told her that they could not help because they were already representing Louis. They suggested that she go to court and plead with the judge to appoint a lawyer for her. Her state child welfare worker refused to become involved because Louis also was a a long-term client of that agency.

The need for free or low-cost legal services in family courts is growing (Johnson 2000). Negotiating family court without representation or support would be challenging for a highly educated person with many resources. For a client like Sharon, who is young and has limited resources, it is likely to be frustrating and confusing, and she can expect to receive little help or tolerance from court personnel. One way that people experience oppression is through systemic deprivation (Hanna, Talley, and Guindon 2000). Sharon has been oppressed by the child welfare system and now faces oppression through inadequate access to legal advocacy. This situation calls for a social worker to become Sharon's advocate and broker to ensure that she is able to have a voice in family court.

The child is the other party in this case whose interests may not be adequately considered. The rules governing the appointment of a lawyer to represent a child vary from state to state, but social workers should lobby for children to be represented in all contested custody cases. In the conservative political climate that has gripped the United States in recent years, public funding for legal representation of the poor has eroded. This has created inequities in family court outcomes, with those able to afford an attorney having a decided advantage in negotiating the process. This disparity represents economic, gender, and age discrimination, and state legislatures across the country need to address it.

BEST INTERESTS OF THE CHILD

Since Goldstein, Freud, and Solnit wrote their enormously influential book, *Beyond the Best Interests of the Child* (1973), courts and lawyers have approached child-related cases by applying the best interests standard. Although this sounds like a way to apply an objective standard to guide a decision, sometimes it reinforces biases and creates a pretext for a decision that a judge favors. Family law practices, developed since the adoption of the best interests standard, have established the interests of the child as paramount and stressed the importance of stability. In addition, the best interests standard supports the analysis of the child's environment to determine its ability to foster social, emotional, cognitive, and moral development (Goldstein, Freud, and Solnit 1973).

Recent research has confirmed the significance of instability in children's development (Moore, Vandivere, and Ehrle 2000). In the child welfare context the concern for consistency and predictability in a child's life has led to legal reforms intended to reduce the amount of time between a child's placement in residential or foster care and the initiation of the legal process to terminate parental rights (The Adoption and Safe Families Act [1997]). In custody cases the ideal of stability for the child has led courts to require a parenting plan to standardize the details of joint custody and visitation arrangements.

The legal principle of best interests of the child reminds courts to consider the effects of a decision on children's lives and to give this consideration priority over any other factors, whether in child welfare, family dissolution, or probate matters. Although having an objective standard for determining best interests may be preferable, the law places the burden on the adversarial process, encouraging each side to argue its case. This model, which prevails elsewhere in the law, is comfortable for lawyers and judges but frequently is not therapeutic for children and families.

LEGAL REPRESENTATION OF CHILDREN

If the adversary process thrives when lawyers zealously advance their position, what can be said about the results of a family case where the children are not represented? Children are the most underrepresented constituents in the legal system (Ventrell 1995). The legal system has not provided extensive resources to provide lawyers for children. Even when lawyers are appointed, they sometimes meet their clients for the first time in court. The determination of best interests requires independent advocacy for the rights and needs of the child. Social workers can facilitate communication with and provide information to a child's attorney.

Most family courts use two types of appointments for children's attorneys. If a lawyer is appointed or hired to represent a child, the lawyer's role is to be a zealous advocate and to advance the wishes of the child client. This includes a duty to maintain confidentiality and a duty to provide competent representation. In some proceedings in family court a judge may appoint a lawyer, or sometimes a nonlawyer, as guardian *ad litem*. In this case the guardian *ad litem* assumes the responsibility of acting in the child's best interests, even if that determination conflicts with the child's wishes. A social worker who disagrees with the position of a child's attorney and feels that the lawyer is not working in the child's best interests can ask the court to appoint a guardian *ad litem,* who can then help the court to recognize the needs of the child. Social workers who are frustrated by the actions of children's lawyers must understand the ethical and practical parameters of this specialized role.

DIVORCE AND CUSTODY

How does society strike a working balance between the desire to allow families to make decisions and the need to protect vulnerable individuals and to provide a structure for registering and enforcing legal arrangements? The adversarial system is ill suited to resolving family issues, and legal professionals have limited backgrounds to forge positive solutions. When the system assumes that a winner and a loser will be the result, it mischaracterizes the needs and ignores the interests of the child. Most divorces do not end up with multiple restraining orders and legal fees that drain every available dollar. Most child custody arrangements do not end up in repeated court interventions and constant turmoil. However, enough divorces do end up increasing the conflict that reformers have begun to respond with increased interdisciplinary staffing of family courts and the use of alternative dispute-resolution strategies.

The majority of the litigation in divorce and custody cases is conducted through motions. One side will make a motion, such as a request for a protective order, referral for a custody evaluation, or change in a visitation schedule, and the other side will file a response. When one side fails to comply with a court order, the opposing side often responds with a motion that asks the court to find the first party in contempt of court. The judge may hold a hearing and rule on the motion. The formality of the proceedings ensures that each party has notice of all actions and an opportunity to respond and to be heard on the motion. (In some cases a lawyer may make a motion that asks the court to decide without waiting for an adversarial hearing. Unfortunately, the formality designed to protect the legal rights of each party creates a system where each party needs a lawyer.

The family law issues in divorce and custody are too numerous to detail here. Social workers need to understand the legal principles that guide the process, the opportunities for advocacy and education, and the need to avoid roles that exacerbate the iatrogenic effects of family court. For example, social workers serving as therapists or as custody evaluators for the courts often are asked to testify about the child's best interests. These professionals risk fueling conflict when they assume the role of advocate rather than collaboratively reaching for problem resolution (Johnson 2000). In preparing court reports, social workers may feel the need to take a side, to be an advocate for the parent who has brought the child to therapy. Sometimes advocacy is necessary, but too often social workers repeat the statements of one parent as evidence against the other parent. In addition, social workers who fail to understand the need to remain family centered may restrict the flow of information crucial to the court. In the name of confidentiality, communication with all relevant parties in a custody case may be limited, unnecessarily hindering collaborative resolution (Johnston 2000).

How does a social worker respond when a child expresses anger, hatred, rejection, or fear toward one parent? The adversarial process encourages the litigation of this issue. Is the child's attitude the result of one parent's brainwashing through repeated negative statements about the other? This process has been called parental alienation syndrome. If the other parent is able to prove parental alienation through the testimony of mental health providers or experts, changes in custody may result. On the other hand, if a child's feelings or attitudes about a parent are based on legitimate responses to inappropriate or dangerous behaviors, it is important to safeguard the child and not allow further trauma. This issue can assume political undertones and lead to an obfuscation of truth. Social workers can lead the legal system to understand that a child's alienation from a parent occurs for a variety of reasons, with a range of intensity. It requires careful assessment and coordinated case management rather than simplistic accusations of culpability (Schepard 2001).

Social workers need to be informed about the rights of parents in divorce situations. For example, each parent has the legal right to consent to medical treatment, to receive copies of educational or medical records, and to continue to be involved in decisions about a child unless a court has ruled otherwise. When faced with a parent who objects to the actions of the other, a social worker should request documentation of court orders. Parents retain discretion in decisions about visitation with grandparents or other significant adults such as ex-partners, although statutes in some states have granted nonparents the right to petition a court for visitation. The Supreme Court has limited these statutes by ruling that such laws must not interfere with the rights of fit parents to make decisions about their children (*Troxel v. Granville* [2000]).

The loss of money, privacy, and control of one's life all characterize current family court experiences. Family decisions should not be made in a context that emphasizes the negative portrayal of other members of the family. Social workers can be a force for change in family court through informed participation in cases and by championing efforts to reform family court interactions so that they are more therapeutic for families.

CHILD ABUSE AND NEGLECT

The authority of the state to protect vulnerable people must be balanced against the privacy right of parents to the care, custody, and control of children. Child welfare is a controversial and often political issue. State laws seem to swing from policies that stress the provision of services to preserve and/or reunify families to vigorous removal and termination of parental rights policies that stress child protection—and back again. Because the issues are politicized and the services are reactive, seldom does meaningful discussion occur about tailoring responses to match a professional social work assessment of the family. Instead, rhetoric about saving children and coddling abusive parents competes with rhetoric about stealing children and denying parents' rights. Judges must make decisions about families within this political maelstrom. The social work orientation of child welfare services has shifted to a litigation-oriented system, which has created a greater need for social workers to build legal knowledge for practice (Briar-Lawson and Drews 2000).

The legal context of child welfare is a mixture of federal and state law. The federal government attaches conditions to its offer to provide funding for state child welfare services. Primary among these is the requirement that states develop a permanent plan for children in state care. The Adoption and Safe Families Act of 1997 requires states to begin proceedings to terminate parental rights when a child has been in placement for fifteen of the previous twenty-two months (103). In addition, the statute identifies some circumstances that allow a judge to authorize that planning for a permanent placement begin immediately. The purpose of these requirements is to reduce the amount of time that a child spends in state care, often drifting from one foster care setting to another. In addition, the quicker pace of termination proceedings makes it more likely that someone will adopt these children because they have been freed for adoption at an earlier age.

To balance parental rights and the state's interest in faster termination proceedings, the federal government also requires states to make reasonable efforts to preserve and reunify the family (except in some circumstances). The federal statute lays out in additional detail what these reasonable efforts are and allows the state to plan for terminating parental rights while attempting to work with the parent (101 (D)).

The role of some lawyers in child protection cases can create conflicts and misunderstandings for social workers. An attorney working for the state is responsible for filing the state's child abuse complaint and representing the position of the state. This is different from any criminal complaint that may be filed as a result of the same set of facts. The child welfare case deals with questions of where the child will reside, who has custody, and what services the child may need. If the action by the parent that gave rise to the child abuse case also violated a criminal statute, the prosecutor may file charges in criminal court. Such charges could range from risk of injury to a minor to assault or rape.

The parent(s) and sometimes grandparents or other interested parties all may have lawyers involved in a case. Too often social workers are not careful in determining which party each lawyer represents and how that affects confidentiality questions. A lawyer appointed for a child generally has the right to access records and speak to any party but should always provide documentation to the social worker of the appointment as the child's lawyer.

As in other areas of the law that I have already discussed, a competent lawyer gathers facts and develops a theory of the case. Applying the legal standards to the facts brings the issues into greater focus and makes them easier to manage. This narrowing of the issues often causes communication problems with social workers who, by nature and training, seek a more inclusive process and solutions that embrace the broader environment. Many lawyers in child welfare cases prepare each case with the intention of winning. This orientation also causes conflicts with social workers, whose focus is developing creative and collaborative problem-solving processes.

The elements that are decisive in a child welfare case include the specific wording of the state statute covering grounds for which the state may remove a child and seek termination of parental rights. A lawyer must prepare to argue the facts against the specific grounds listed in the statute. Second, states must demonstrate that they made reasonable efforts to preserve or reunify the family. A lawyer may argue that services were not available or that the state failed to help a parent in some meaningful way. Finally, the parent's lawyer could argue that the state failed to prove its case. In terminating parental rights, states must prove all necessary elements by the standard of clear and convincing evidence.

The result of legal thinking in the context of a legal proceeding is that issues become narrow. An attorney may not be interested in an issue that a social worker considers salient, if it does not fit into the theory of the case. Because child welfare workers prepare the documentation that the court uses to determine parental fitness, social work practice is infused with legal ramifications. Social workers in child welfare must be knowledgeable about federal and state statutes and provide the court with relevant, unbiased, and accurate information. Social workers asked to testify should prepare by quizzing the attorney for the state about the specific goals for their testimony so that they can be more effective.

State laws govern the reporting of child abuse. All social workers are considered to be mandated reporters if they have a reasonable suspicion that a child is at risk or has been abused or neglected. State laws generally grant social workers immunity for the good-faith reporting of child abuse. In several cases parents have sought to bypass this immunity by filing malpractice lawsuits against social workers and other mental health providers, claiming that a negligent assessment led to the report and that this caused harm to the parent (see, for example, *Bird v. W.C.W.* [1994]). The behavior of a social worker must reach an exceptional level of culpability to overcome the usual rule protecting social workers who report child abuse suspicions (Madden 1998).

Child welfare historically has been a social work–dominated profession (Briar-Lawson and Drews 2000). As the system has evolved, courts have become more concerned about the rights of the individual parties, and the procedures have become more formal and more contentious. The positive aspect of this legal orientation has been the opportunity to use legal protections to force a state to prove its case before taking action to remove a child or break up a family. The negative aspect is that the courts have used the adversarial system to make family decisions based on the arguments of individual constituents. The courts frequently use a medical model of practice that highlights deficits (S. Brooks 1999). Social workers should work to reclaim child welfare practice and to work for legal reforms that will make the courts more therapeutic for children and families while protecting the rights of all parties.

THE PROCESS AND ORIENTATION OF PROBATE COURT

Social workers are most concerned about those probate matters that relate to competency and the protection of vulnerable clients. Probate courts manage legal issues that might occur in a person's life course such as assigning guardianship, granting approval for and monitoring medical and financial powers of attorney, implementing the final wishes of a person by processing wills, and overseeing the distribution of estates.

The probate court system in the United States has evolved from the English ecclesiastical and equity courts (National Center 1999). Local and state officials developed rules and structures for probate courts that reflected the needs and customs of each state. As a result, the evolution of probate courts has varied by state. Some jurisdictions developed a separate probate court system. Some states do not distinguish probate matters from any other legal matter, granting jurisdiction to the local district court. Finally, some states have given responsibility for probate matters to particular judges or specialized units within courts of broader jurisdiction (National Center 1999).

Probate courts vary in the subject matter under their jurisdiction. In addition to traditional probate matters, such as guardianships, wills, trusts and estates, some courts handle mundane legal chores such as registering a name change, processing minor offenses, and issuing marriage licenses. Most probate court systems share a commitment to community-based, accessible legal services. Generally, a person with business before the probate court does not need an attorney, although most people find comfort in being represented by legal counsel. The language, procedures, and orientation of probate courts focus on individual and family matters that are usually less contentious than a criminal or civil matter. Because of this, probate courts tend to be more personal in many jurisdictions, although these courts too have clear procedures and rules to protect the rights and interests of all parties. Many probate matters involve constitutional liberty interests, requiring probate court judges to ensure due process.

Social workers have the opportunity to be influential in ensuring that court decisions respect clients' rights and help clients to maintain self-determination.

However, equally important is protecting clients from abuse at the hands of family, friends, and the probate court system. At times, an effort to have a person declared incompetent is related to a desire to control that person's assets. Sometimes the intent of people petitioning the court is unimpeachable but conflicts with the wishes of the individual whom they are trying to protect. Unfortunately, the system that probate courts in some jurisdictions use to appoint estate lawyers and guardians has been a closed system of political connections, kickbacks, and unconscionable fees (R. Stein 1997).

Several legal concepts govern decision making in probate matters. Social workers who understand these concepts can be more effective in advocating for safe and productive outcomes to the probate process. For example, if a client objects to the appointment of a guardian, or is contesting a probate court matter, the court may be able to appoint a lawyer to represent the person. However, sometimes this requires effective advocacy by professionals on behalf of the client. Social workers should understand the differences in the types of arrangements for protecting the interests of those with functional impairments.

Probate judges review proposed arrangements for the care of people with functional limitations that affect their decision-making capacity. These limitations may be the result of age or a disabling condition caused by mental illness, developmental disability, accident, or illness. The standard for the probate court is whether a person has the ability to make decisions (competency) and whether the person is at risk of harm and thus needs supervision. Probate judges assess competency with reference to the demands of a particular task. For example, a person may have a disability that impairs the ability to manage financial affairs but still is fully competent to make medical decisions (Madden 1998).

The probate judge is responsible for protecting not only the person but also the person's rights. Because of this the judge has a responsibility to require legitimate evidence provided by qualified professionals regarding a person's ability to make decisions and function independently. Second, the judge should assess the opportunity for the least intrusive alternative, including the use of limited guardianships and the inclusion of social service programs to support self-determination (National Center 1999:standard 3.3.1.0). For example, government programs may require recipients of benefits to have a guardian appointed as a representative or protective payee, but this guardianship might be limited to the management of this benefit.

In probate matters the judge provides a substitute decision maker for an incapacitated or incompetent person. The system is based on the ability to trust the person who is given the power. A fiduciary relationship requires honesty, avoidance of conflicts of interest, the time and ability to perform the associated tasks, and a strong commitment to the person (National Center 1999:standard 3.1.2). A fiduciary must place the interests of the person above any personal or political interests. Probate courts are required to monitor all fiduciaries and to protect the assets and interests of the person. This is done by requiring fiduciaries to make regular reports to the probate court detailing all transactions and decisions. While all probate appointments carry a fiduciary responsibility, the level of power granted to make decisions for the person varies according to the needs of the situation.

A guardian is given the right to make decisions for a person (ward) under the supervision of the probate court. A court orders a guardianship when it finds a person incompetent to safely or effectively manage life decisions. The goal for the probate judge is to identify the proper balance between the preservation of the individual's independence, the need to protect the person's assets, and the necessity of making life decisions on behalf of the ward (Pettit 2001).

Conservatorship is a voluntary process whereby a person asks the probate court to appoint a specific individual to manage her or his estate. A probate court must find that the person making the request is competent to understand the ramifications of the request. The court must also assess whether the individual is capable of making the decision while being incapable of managing financial affairs.

Two people can make a contract giving one party the authority to make decisions for the other party. This contract, called a power of attorney, can cover financial, placement, or medical decisions. Social workers can help people to plan for their future needs by carefully drafting legal forms. Some states permit residents to make a springing power of attorney. For example, a parent who is HIV positive may set up a springing power of attorney, which grants guardianship rights to a trusted friend and is to take effect upon incapacitation or death of the parent. Most contracts are written as durable powers of attorney, meaning that the power of attorney remains in effect after the person becomes incapacitated, eliminating the need to return to court to seek the appointment of a guardian.

One strategy for allowing people's expressed preferences to guide decision making is to create advance directives detailing the types of treatment for which the individual would consent. Hospitals and nursing homes supply these advance directive forms and may be part of the making of a will. Recently, some states have begun to allow advance directives specifically for mental health, allowing people, while competent, to determine which types of treatment they consent to in the event that they are no longer able to make competent decisions (Rosenfeld 2001). Advance directives provide evidence of a person's wishes but may be challenged by family members and may be overridden by courts if the court finds the person lacked capacity to make the decision initially or if current circumstances convince a judge to order treatment (Winick 1991). Social work roles do not end with assisting clients to prepare advance directives. People need advocates to support their right to make treatment decisions. If an advance directive is challenged, social workers should be prepared to testify regarding a person's competency at the time that the advance directive was prepared.

JUDICIAL RESPONSES TO SOCIAL PROBLEMS

Probate court and family court are examples of specialized courts that manage legal issues common to social work clients. There is a growing movement to develop other specialized courts to respond to social problems such as domestic violence and drug abuse. The benefit of specialized courts is the level of expertise and the multidisciplinary staff that can respond to the unique needs of these situations. Many specialized courts are emerging from the therapeutic jurisprudence movement. The effort to increase the therapeutic effect of the court process on the individual is intended to reduce recidivism and improve outcomes. The role of the judge in specialized courts is nontraditional, collaborative, and focused on problem solving. In traditional adversarial litigation the role of the judge is more limited and formal, applying legal rules that often reflect a punitive agenda. The frustration with traditional approaches to serious social problems has fueled the reform efforts.

DRUG COURTS

In 1989 Miami became the first jurisdiction to experiment with drug courts. This initial drug court targeted people who had been arrested for the first time on relatively low-level felony drug offenses (Goldkamp 2000). These courts have spread to many jurisdictions in recent years. The programs screen prospective defendants, with most drug courts accepting only nonviolent drug offenders and those whose criminal activity was related to drug use. These cases are diverted from the traditional adjudication path in criminal court if the defendants agree to participate in drug treatment. Upon successful completion of treatment defendants are rewarded with dismissal of their cases. Instead of prison sentences, these courts offer counseling, addiction treatment, drug use monitoring, and closely supervised probation. Because of the experience with the dynamics of drug abuse, the court deals with relapses as part of the court's treatment process. However, failure to comply with the interventions of a drug court can result in criminal sanctions.

Some defense attorneys object to the idea of a treatment team and are concerned that their clients' legal rights may be compromised. For example, the drug court may encourage a defendant to admit to a relapse because acknowledging it fosters honesty, collaboration, and a treatment focus. However, a subsequent relapse or re-arrest may trigger the criminal sanctions, including incarceration. Alternatively, plea bargaining or actively contesting the offense may have a better legal outcome for the client from the perspective of the defense attorney (Quinn 2000–2001). Representing people in drug court takes a very different mind-set. These courts discourage the traditional adversarial approaches and encourage defense attorneys to become part of the team supporting the client.

DOMESTIC VIOLENCE COURTS

In recent years many states have developed model domestic violence programs. These programs emend the focus of the court's attention from the purely punitive response, applying criminal sanctions to the abusive partner, to a multidisciplinary, service-oriented approach for victims and children, combined with required treatment for offenders and strict monitoring of compliance with protective orders (Tsai 2000). Domestic violence courts are concerned with issues of victim advocacy and support, perpetrator accountability and monitoring, and general mental health concerns of all parties (Tsai 2000).

The key feature of these specialized courts and the concomitant law reforms is that they incorporate the dynamics of domestic violence. For example, some states have taken the decision to prosecute a domestic violence offense out of the hands of the victim. The crime is considered a crime against the state. The overwhelming message of the courts is intolerance for family violence. Traditional courts regarded victims merely as witnesses, limited their sanctions to the wagging fingers of stern-faced judges whose basic belief was that what happened within a family was not the business of others. Society did not consider the courts the place to manage social service and mental health needs. Legal systems have begun to recognize the importance of responding to the complex needs of families affected by domestic violence with a combination of legal, social, mental health, and community services.

Social workers have been at the forefront of movements to create specialized courts and to work for legal reforms that meet the needs of real people with real problems. Legal reforms of juvenile, family, probate, and other specialized courts have resulted in improved services, but no one has conducted the empirical research needed to demonstrate the improved efficiency of specialized courts over traditional legal approaches. Social workers must appreciate the legal principles that protect the rights of individuals in order to be effective participants in these settings.

8.

TORTS: HOW THE LAW PROVIDES COMPENSATION
FOR INJURY AND DETERS UNSAFE PRACTICES

> When a man's life is destroyed or damaged by some wound or privation
> of soul or body, which is due to other men's actions or negligence, it is not
> only his sensibility that suffers but also his aspiration toward the good.
> —Simone Weil

A TORT IS AN ACTION (or sometimes omission) committed by an individual or entity that violates a standard of reasonable behavior and causes harm to another party. The primary purpose of tort law is to compensate people for losses that result from the behavior of the defendant. As I discussed in chapter 3, some torts also may be crimes, but the punishment for a crime is a public sanction such as a fine or a jail term, a response that often does not include making the injured victim whole. As a result, it is common for a person to file a civil suit to seek to recover damages, even if the state has filed a criminal complaint.

The three major categories of torts are negligence, intentional acts, and strict liability. Negligence torts are the most familiar to social workers. Negligence involves the failure to act reasonably in a given set of circumstances. Malpractice, the negligence of professionals, has been applied to the conduct of social workers who fail to meet the applicable standard of care. Intentional torts involve behaviors such as libel, assault, trespass, and intentional infliction of emotional distress. Finally, tort law holds companies strictly liable for the manufacture of defective products, which means that an injured party does not have to prove that the defect resulted from the company's failure to follow an industry norm or standard.

The purposes of a tort lawsuit are to compensate an injured party and to deter unreasonable or unsafe behavior. When careless, reckless, or intentional actions cause injuries, the tort system makes people and corporations accountable for their behavior (Buckley 1993). In addition to these primary goals, the tort system has discreet instrumental goals such as promoting economic efficiency (Landes and Posner 1987), encouraging all people to create a safer society (Buckley 1993), and pushing technological progress by demanding higher standards from industries.

A popular debate is the legitimacy of tort lawsuits. Those seeking to play legal lottery do commit abuses, but the overwhelming effect of tort law is to make it too costly for individuals and industries to act unreasonably or unsafely. Most high-profile, excessive damage awards are the exceptions, and appellate courts reduce many of these. Social workers have had to examine their practice approaches and tailor their practice policies to reduce the risk of lawsuits. The real effect of this incentive is to make practice safer and more effective. It has encouraged the development of best practices that are based on empirical research on outcomes (Madden 1998). Social workers have participated in workshops and courses on legal issues, and scholars have encouraged their schools of social work to expand the legal content in the curriculum (Madden 2000). Tort law plays an integral part in social work practice, making knowledge of the essential elements of this area of the law imperative.

Oliver Wendell Holmes is credited with developing much of the structure of tort law. His theory of torts relied on the idea that in a free society, an individual who causes harm to another should be required to compensate the injured person for damages. Holmes's analytic model found liability when a defendant could have, or should have, foreseen the possibility of harm and therefore could have acted differently in order to avoid causing the harm (D. Rosenberg 1995). This line of reasoning helps to ensure that justice is served in sorting out responsibility for injuries. Several essential elements to a negligence claim have emerged from Holmes's principles. Lawyers think about torts in terms of these elements and organize evidence in order to evaluate the strength of a case.

ELEMENTS OF NEGLIGENCE AND MALPRACTICE ACTIONS

The primary elements of a negligence claim are a duty of care owed by one party to the other, a breach of that duty, an injury to the victim caused by the breach, foreseeability of the injury, and the existence of damage to the victim (Buckley 1993). The following case, involving a lawsuit against a social worker and her agency, serves as an example for examining the primary elements of a negligence tort claim.

Jane was a client of a clinical social worker in a mental health clinic. Some time after she ended treatment, Jane learned that a medical records clerk employed by the mental health clinic had improperly released confidential information about Jane to a third party without her consent. Jane sued the agency, clinical social worker, and clerk. She claimed that the disclosure of the information was negligent and constituted malpractice.

In a negligence lawsuit a court can determine the existence of a duty to act reasonably toward others in several ways. Each person owes a duty of ordinary prudence to others (Shapo 1999). Sometimes this is referred to as the reasonable person standard. Courts determine whether someone violated a duty of care by examining the circumstances, evaluating the reasonableness of the behavior, and comparing it to what an ordinary person would have done. When a special or professional relationship exists between the parties, the duty of care rises to the level expected for a person in that position. In Jane's lawsuit the social worker and agency have an obvious duty to their clients. The Supreme Court has protected confidentiality, viewing it as an indispensable component of mental health treatment, which is "a public good of transcendent importance" (*Jaffe v. Redmond*, 518 U.S. 1, 11 [1998]). A person who enters counseling has an expectation that the information from this experience will be kept private. This expectation, along with professional standards articulated in ethical codes, professional publications, and state statutes, gives rise to a duty to maintain confidentiality.

The foreseeability that others could be harmed by the breach determines the scope of the duty. Suppose that the information released by the clerk involved Jane's exploration of her sexual orientation. Is it foreseeable that the release of this information could cause harm to Jane's husband? A creative lawyer could easily argue that the agency owed a duty of confidentiality to the husband. Social workers need to be aware of this principle, as it may be the critical issue in cases where a client's family members file third-party complaints. The cases involving recovered memory have addressed a number of issues related to third-party liability but not always in a consistent manner (Madden and Parody 1997). A lawyer's questioning may focus on developing proof of duty and analyzing the foreseeability of harm to the third party.

Referencing legislative standards or industry practice is the only way to determine whether professional behavior was unreasonable and thereby constituted a breach of duty. Often negligence lawsuits feature the testimony of expert witnesses to explain the professional standard of care to the court. A lawyer may also ask the expert to give an opinion about whether a breach of the standard of care occurred, given the circumstances of the case.

In the example case the defense lawyer could question whether the social worker and the agency are responsible for the independent actions of a non-professional clerk. The doctrine of *respondeat superior* holds that an employer is responsible for the negligence that employees commit while engaged in the scope of their work. Alternatively, the court might find the agency negligent for failing to properly train or supervise the clerk. Either way, the agency is unlikely to escape its liability by claiming that it had no duty to the client. The social worker, however, might be successful in arguing that her behavior did not violate any standards and may petition the court to dismiss her from the lawsuit.

Even if a breach of a duty has occurred, a defendant is not liable for the victim's injuries unless the defendant caused the harm. Causation may be direct or indirect (Buckley 1993). The analysis of direct causation is often called "but-for causation" (but for the defendant's actions, the plaintiff would not have been injured). Indirect causation can be difficult to prove. Did the release of the confidential information cause Jane's marriage to break up? This claim may turn on evidence concerning the state of the marriage before the release of the information.

For Jane's case to succeed, the court must find that her injuries were the natural and probable consequence of the defendant's behavior (proximate cause). Was the injury reasonably foreseeable in the way that Holmes explained was necessary to a finding of liability? Jane's complaint against the social worker argued that the clinical record contained too much personal information that was not directly related to the goals of her treatment. Because of this the clerk had access to the highly confidential information and subsequently released this without consent. Was the clinician's record keeping a proximate cause of Jane's injury? Could the clinician have foreseen that writing a case note about Jane's sexual identity issue would lead to terrible consequences if it became known? Would the analysis change if the social worker worked for the military and Jane was in the service, given the "don't ask, don't tell" policy?

Clearly, the inclusion of the information in the social worker's notes caused the harm to Jane, but the social worker has no liability unless including the information in the file was also the proximate cause of the harm. These issues would have to be argued at trial, but the illustration helps to make the point that the element of proximate cause can be determinative in a negligence suit.

DAMAGES

Damages refer to the amount of money to be provided to the plaintiff in a successful tort suit. The two categories of damage are compensatory and punitive. Compensatory damages, also referred to as actual damages, provide money for direct costs and losses suffered by the plaintiff. In some cases damages to a plaintiff are difficult to prove. In the case example, Jane would need to document the injuries that she suffered because of the breach. In mental health practice a plaintiff may find quantifying the damages to be difficult. How much is emotional pain and suffering worth? How does a monetary award compensate a person for a divorce?

Lawyers will sometimes construct a set of standard responses to emotional trauma such as loss of sleep and appetite and constantly feeling anxious, distracted, depressed, or isolated, affecting general health and job performance. Jane's lawyer might argue that these symptoms are permanent because, once released, the confidential information cannot be recalled. An attorney might place a dollar value on this ongoing pain and suffering of $100 a day and consult actuarial tables to determine Jane's life expectancy. In this way the lawyer could construct a damage figure that would provide a model for the jury to understand.

In some intentional torts and where gross negligence is involved, a plaintiff has an opportunity to be awarded punitive damages. In Jane's case she may be able to seek punitive damages from the clerk if Jane sued the clerk, alleged intentional infliction of emotional distress, and was able to demonstrate that the clerk released the confidential information intentionally and with malice. In some cases state statutes specify when a plaintiff may seek punitive damages or receive treble actual damages.

DEFENSES TO NEGLIGENCE

In addition to the defenses to each element of negligence that I have already reviewed, other legal strategies to mitigate liability are available. Contributory negligence is a defense that argues that the plaintiff's own negligence contributed to the injuries. The theoretical assumption is that each person has a duty of reasonable care to self. Historically, the effect of demonstrating that the plaintiff contributed to the injury was to exonerate the defendant (Buckley 1993). In recent times this policy has changed to comparative negligence: The court reduces the damage award by the percentage of responsibility for the injury attributable to the plaintiff's negligence. The jury must assess the relative responsibility of the parties in its deliberation of the case.

One defense to a negligence case is based on the statute of limitations. This is the statute that defines the maximum time available for an aggrieved party to file a lawsuit. The time limits vary according to the type of complaint; in some cases that means that lawyers will have to demonstrate how a case that sounds like a negligence case is really a contract violation (because the deadline has passed for filing the negligence case, but the contracts deadline has not passed). Another defense, sovereign immunity, is a direct descendant of the English principle that a king cannot be sued. In this country government employees initially were protected from all suits, but this shelter has been reduced in recent years. Several other defenses to negligence suits have been explored in previous examples, including lack of jurisdiction and affirmative defenses (chapter 6).

Sovereign immunity still protects some public officials from lawsuits because of the nature of their roles. Legislators, judges, and prosecutors, for example, enjoy absolute immunity from suits related to their official duties. Other officials, most notably child welfare workers, are generally considered to have qualified immunity for actions taken in good faith, although in some jurisdictions child welfare workers have absolute immunity. Some critics argue that qualified immunity is sufficient to preserve the freedom of judgment and decision making that is crucial to those practicing in child welfare (Gifford 1995). Qualified immunity does allow an injured party to sue if the government official intentionally acted to cause harm. In the child welfare context a worker who lied, misrepresented facts, or otherwise acted in bad faith might be subject to a lawsuit.

INTENTIONAL TORTS

The second category of personal injury law involves behavior that is intended to cause harm to another party. Although less significant to social work practice, social workers may become involved with several types of claims. All intentional torts have two required elements, behavior with intent to harm and a resulting injury (Buckley 1993). Intentional infliction of emotional distress is a claim that the defendant's extreme and outrageous conduct intentionally or recklessly caused severe emotional distress (Restatement (Second) of Torts 46 [1965]). The judgment of whether a behavior reaches the level of being extreme and outrageous is often the key issue, and courts generally apply subjective criteria in reaching a decision. A judge must balance individual freedom, especially freedom of speech and action, with the need to impute responsibility for an injury suffered as a direct result of an intentional act (Shapo 1999). For example, consider the case of a gay rights activist who announces that a prominent community leader is gay. If the community leader sues, should a court find the activist's actions to be extreme and outrageous if the leader is in fact gay?

Clients may accuse social workers of the torts of fraud or misrepresentation in relationship to diagnosis and communications with managed-care and insurance companies. These torts involve intentionally false statements made to obtain payment or to deceive. Further, a client may sue a social worker for defamation related to statements or written communications. Social workers should maintain their clinical records with attention to the possibility that statements that clients have made about other individuals may some day become public and cause a defamation lawsuit.

BENEFITS TO SOCIAL WORK PRACTICE

Tort law provides a means of social control by enforcing responsibility and assigning the payment of damages for injuries (D. Rosenberg 1995). Social workers participating in a tort case must have an understanding of the essential elements of the case and the role of their testimony in proving or disproving the elements. Many clients have had their rights violated and have been injured by the negligence or intentional acts of others. Social workers can become more effective advocates when they understand the principles and processes of the tort system.

The development of the common law through court decisions helps social workers to understand the expectations for appropriate professional behavior. Without a tort system, would social workers have a duty to warn? How could clients who have been harmed by incompetent or inappropriate practice be compensated for their injuries without the opportunity to seek redress in the courts? The tendency for social workers is to think of malpractice in terms of risk reduction. Do certain diagnoses increase the risk of being sued? Are there forms that social workers can use to disclaim liability? These issues are important to examine but ultimately are insufficient. Legally safe practice emerges from professionally competent practice. Familiarity with assessment and treatment planning options, maintaining quality supervision, documenting practice, adhering to practice management policies, and acting in consonance with professional ethics are the basic elements of safe practice. The tort system is society's mechanism for encouraging safe and effective practice by all professionals.

9

CONTRACTS AND OTHER LEGAL ISSUES IN THE MANAGEMENT OF SOCIAL WORK PRACTICE

That whatever a man says, promises, or resolves in passion, he must stick to later on when he is cold and sober. This demand is among the heaviest burdens that weigh on humankind. —Friedrich Nietzsche

BASIC PRINCIPLES OF CONTRACT LAW

Legal rules can create efficient ways of enabling the transfer of goods and services and, in some cases, for binding people to the promises that they make. Contract law in the United States has evolved from a formal, commercially based discipline into a flexible, broadly based field (Posner 1999). It structures the relationships between private parties in a manner that courts can enforce. Social workers encounter issues of contract in employment, managed care, and even family matters, such as surrogacy and prenuptial agreements. Understanding the basic elements of an enforceable contract is indispensable for participation in modern society.

In the past, courts allowed nearly unlimited freedom to contract. During the twentieth century, courts became more active in limiting contractual arrangements that violate public policy and gave more equality to consumers and other groups with less power in the contracting process (Slawson 1996). For example, consider a lease for an apartment in a run-down building. The lease requires a damage deposit of two months' rent and stipulates that the tenant will forfeit the deposit if he or she moves out before the end of the two-year lease period. If the property owner negligently allows the boiler to remain unrepaired during a cold stretch, causing the tenant to move out before the end of the lease period, enforcing the contract and allowing forfeiture of the damage deposit would be unjust. Modern contract law has evolved in a manner that ensures a balancing of fairness and predictability in the making of formal agreements (Hillman 1997).

The primary ingredients of a contract are the offer and the acceptance. The legal question in many contract cases is whether the parties have actually entered into a contract. This may seem self-evident, but the intent of the parties may be an issue. Did the two sides come to a meeting of the minds concerning the contract? When courts examine controversies in the offer and the acceptance, they generally apply the reasonable person standard, similar to the test in negligence cases. Courts may examine the language used in the discussions and the actions taken in response to the circumstances. To help determine intent, courts also analyze language that is common to certain transactions. The key point of analysis is whether both parties understood that they were making a commitment to take some action. Courts have a number of remedies that they can impose to ensure a fair outcome in those cases in which they find that one party is liable for violating the terms of a contract.

The second essential element of a contract is called *consideration*. This is the benefit or the detriment that one party experiences as a result of understanding that it has entered into a contract (Vandevelde 1998). Consideration can be in the form of money spent or actions initiated by a party. For example, an experienced clinical supervisor agrees to provide two hours of supervision on the first and third Monday of each month to a private practice social worker in return for a fee of $150 per month. The supervisor turns down the opportunity to run a parent-training seminar because it would conflict with the time promised for the supervision. On the day the supervision is to begin, the clinician changes his mind and decides to engage another supervisor. Should the contract be enforced? If so, how would a court arrive at a just outcome? Should a court require the social worker to honor the agreement by participating in supervision and paying the agreed-upon rate, or should the social worker pay some amount of damages to the supervisor? Would the supervisor's detrimental reliance on the promise (turning down another opportunity) be sufficient to have completed the contract? Suppose the supervisor was able to contact the agency sponsoring the parenting group and was offered the position at the same or higher rate of pay than she would have received by doing the supervision?

These questions raise the essential issues in many basic contract cases: What factors create a duty to fulfill a contract? At what point in a negotiation is an obligation produced? Must contracts be written and signed in order to be valid? Does the signing of a contract ever not constitute an enforceable agreement?

When an equitable rationale for enforcing a promise is available, such as consideration or reasonable detrimental reliance, courts generally are inclined to enforce the contract. The related analysis, however, is whether one party suffered any injury as a result of the breach of contract. The courts generally do not enforce a contract between two parties when neither party reasonably relied on the promise or acted to its detriment. As a policy matter, the position of the two sides is no different position than before the aborted agreement. In addition, courts generally will not enforce a promise by one party made without anticipation of any action by the other party, such as a promise to give a gift (e.g., "If I win the lottery tonight, I will give you half").

LIABILITY FOR BREACH OF CONTRACT

The initial analysis of a contract focuses on formation of an effective contract. Was an offer made and an acceptance conveyed? When the determination is that a contract exists, the analysis shifts to the elements that create liability for a breach of contract. When a lawyer examines a contract case, three primary elements determine liability. Was there a breach of a promise? Did the plaintiff suffer a loss? Was the loss a direct result of the breach? This analysis is similar in structure and function to the analysis of a tort and, in fact, the two legal theories have many connections.

A party is considered to have committed a breach if the agreed-upon action is not completed. However, courts will examine whether the partial performance of a promise constitutes a material breach. For example, in the landlord-tenant case discussed earlier in this chapter, suppose the lease requires the owner to return the security deposit within ten days of the tenant's vacating the premises. The property owner resists, arguing that he deserves to keep the deposit because the tenant moved out prematurely. The owner finally refunds the deposit after two weeks. Courts would probably find this to be a minor inconvenience, not material to the essential elements of the lease contract, and would be unlikely to intervene. The courts also may base the decision not to intervene on the related issue of loss.

Modern contract law tends to require a monetary injury in order to find liability. Disappointment and outrage are insufficient injuries to create liability in most contract cases. Parties to a contract sometimes include in the contract wording that addresses how they will handle a breach, should it occur. The parties may determine the amount of damages to be paid if one party does not perform. These arrangements are called liquidated damage clauses. Some contracts, for example, specify that 10 percent will be added to any unpaid portion of an amount owed under a contract. The courts will enforce these clauses if they are reasonable.

An important limitation on the issue of loss is the determination of whether the loss occurred as a direct result of the breach of contract. The analysis rests on the concept of fairness and examines whether the injury was foreseeable at the time of the breach. In the supervision example, let us change the facts such that the supervisor was the party who breached the contract. When she was offered the opportunity to run the parenting group, she reneged on her promise to provide supervision to the social worker. Instead, the social worker found a replacement supervisor who subsequently released confidential information concerning one of the social worker's clients. The social worker was sued and lost a major judgment in court. One could argue that the original supervisor's breach of contract led to the events that culminated in a monetary injury for the social worker. However, the relationship between the breach and the loss is not direct. The misbehavior of the second supervisor was the direct cause of the injury to the social worker. A court would be unlikely to find contract liability for the first supervisor in this instance.

Some scholars believe that earlier forms of contract law gave preference to freedom, both the freedom to make contracts and the freedom to be free from government intrusion into voluntary agreements (Slawson 1996). Although courts continue to respect freedom of contract, the primary value of contract law is fairness. If someone makes a promise and then breaches the promise, causing injury to another person, contract law is invoked to fashion an outcome that is fair and just. This means that not every contract is enforced the way it was originally conceived. Courts do enforce verbal contracts where evidence exists of a legitimate agreement, although the law requires some transactions to be in writing.

Some basic defenses to a breach of contract are available. One party may claim that circumstances have changed or that it made a mistake in forming the contract or in judging the conditions, resulting in a situation where performance of the contract would either be impossible or would result in a significant loss. Courts may accept evidence of changed circumstances to excuse the performance of a contract in order to protect economic efficiency. It would be unjust to allow one party to receive the benefit and the other party to assume the cost of changed circumstances. When fraud, duress, or coercion are involved in the making of a contract, courts may excuse a party from liability and void a contract. When the two parties to a contract have a vast disparity in power, courts may consider one party as not having freely agreed to all the provisions of a contract. Courts may void contracts of this sort based on fairness and public policy reasons.

The damages available to plaintiffs who are successful in demonstrating a breach of contract by the defendant are more limited than those available in tort actions. The categories of damages include compensatory damages (direct monetary losses suffered as a result of the breach) and in some cases the related costs that arise as a consequence of the breach. Because the goal of contract law is fairness, it does not punish the breaching side with responsibility beyond the direct effects of the breach, nor does contract law enrich the plaintiff beyond the actual injury.

CONTRACTS WITH CLIENTS: INFORMED CONSENT

Social workers and their clients enter into a contract when they form a treatment relationship. Social workers do not usually think of practice policies and fee agreements as a contract, but these factors constitute the terms, and a court may rule on breaches of these contracts. The process of informed consent is essential to contract claims. Social workers provide a description of the services to be delivered, along with a review of the policies of the practice. Clients agree to the fee schedule and sign forms allowing the social worker to bill their insurance companies. The analysis of contract liability flows from the offer of services, the acceptance by the client, the provision of services, and the paying of fees. Either party can claim breach of contract— social workers generally allege nonpayment of fees, and clients may allege failure to provide some material element of the services. Sometimes a breach of contract claim may be made as part of, or in place of, a malpractice complaint, especially where the statute of limitations for a tort claim is shorter or where evidence of negligence is difficult to prove.

CONTRACTS WITH MANAGED-CARE ORGANIZATIONS

In the past a fee-for-service model was the norm for mental health practices. Clients, or their insurance companies, would pay for each visit, although most policies placed caps on the total that the company would pay out in any one year and for the life of the policy. Managed-care companies, by contrast, determine the number of sessions that they will cover based on the client's symptoms, diagnosis, and treatment plan. One characteristic of managed care that frustrates and angers practitioners is the powerlessness that most social workers feel in dealing with these large organizations. The managed-care companies' control of the payment system fuels the power that they can exert. Individual practitioners and small groups that are dependent on referrals from these sources are hesitant to object to policies or challenge contract terms aggressively. Treatment decisions often seem to be made on the basis of economics rather than clinical evidence. Balancing professional helping values with corporate values has become increasingly difficult (Shapiro 1995).

Practitioners need to understand the legal ramifications of the contracts that they sign with managed-care organizations. The nature of a contract is that it is an agreement negotiated for the benefit of both parties. The mental health field has been slow to challenge how managed-care companies provide services to clients and the conditions that these companies place on professional practice. As a result, social workers are feeling increasingly disempowered and disillusioned.

A contract between a managed-care company and a social worker is similar to a standard business contract. However, counseling and psychotherapy differ from standard businesses because the "product" is the health of the client (Higuchi and Coscia 1995). Some standard business practices place social workers in an ethically untenable situation. Managed-care contracts often include "no-cause termination" clauses. This provision allows either a provider or the managed-care company to cancel the contract without reason. Unfortunately, managed-care companies have used the clause to drop social workers from preferred provider lists in retaliation for contesting decisions to deny payment for services that the practitioner believes are necessary.

Another controversial provision of the contracts used by many managed-care providers is the "gag," or "no disparagement," provision (Higuchi and Coscia 1995). These clauses prohibit a social worker from discussing the decisions or policies of the managed-care organization. The untenable part of this clause is its use by the company to prohibit a social worker from informing a client about treatment options that the managed-care company would not cover. These clauses also stop a social worker from discussing with the client any level of disagreement with the managed-care organization regarding treatment decisions. This type of infringement of free speech and intrusion into the therapeutic relationship should result in outrage and action by mental health professionals. The decision of most practitioners to continue to enter into such contracts is evidence of the disparity in power between the managed-care organizations and the providers. Some states have taken action to eliminate these provisions from managed-care contracts, but social workers should read their agreements carefully before signing.

The written policies of most managed-care companies include

- The process for submitting claims
- The assignment of benefits directly to the provider rather than sending payment to the client
- Billing for missed sessions and direct billing of clients
- Charging clients for uncovered sessions or for the difference between the therapist's usual rate and the amount paid by the insurer
- The handling of co-pays (Yenney and APA 1994)

In all these situations social workers must be knowledgeable about the specific policies of the company. By signing a contract with a managed-care company, the social worker has agreed to abide by the stated conditions. This is why the critical time for examining, questioning, and negotiating the conditions for the provision and reimbursement of services is before signing a contract.

Those managed-care companies that require the charging of co-pays or deductibles often have language in their contracts that require providers to collect the fees. A social worker who routinely waives these charges for clients is in violation of the contract, because this is an important component of a managed-care company's strategy for limiting unnecessary care.

In dealing with clients whose care is managed, social workers must consider how the treatment plan fits with the number of sessions approved by the insurer. If the treatment plan posits goals that are impossible to meet within a limited time, clients may feel pressured to continue treatment beyond the approved number of sessions. Social workers should communicate effectively with care managers and clients and make use of the appeals process where necessary. The safest legal strategy may be to commit to treat clients until the treatment plan is completed or until a nonpaying client can be safely transferred. This protects a worker from abandonment or malpractice charges while avoiding problems with inappropriate billing.

LEGAL ISSUES IN AGENCY MANAGEMENT

Nora was two years out of her M.S.W. program and lightyears from feeling ready to function effectively as an agency administrator. She had concentrated her coursework and practicum experiences in administration and planning, and she had been the executive director of a grassroots program serving runaway youth. Two months earlier Nora started her new job as director of a large regional program that provides a wide range of services to senior citizens. Several weeks after she began work, she found herself locked in a difficult negotiation with the state department of aging to provide case management services. At the same time she was informed about a legal issue regarding an employee of the counseling unit who had been getting poor evaluations from her supervisor for three years. The supervisor wanted to fire the worker but was fearful of being sued. In addition, a member of the clinical staff had received a notice that a former client was considering a malpractice action against him and the agency. The social worker admitted that he had not received regular supervision during the period that he was treating the client in question.

Nora retreated to her private office and celebrated the most significant perks of her new position: a couch, a door that closed, and a secretary to screen her calls. She sat down, sighed heavily, and began to peruse catalogues from programs offering master's degrees in business administration and law school catalogues. She would need an expanded knowledge base to effectively administer this social service agency.

Many practitioners find themselves performing administrative tasks that involve myriad of legal issues for which they are unprepared. Like Nora, they may seek further education or consultation with experts as needs arise. This section introduces some legal issues involved in the administration of a social service agency. Those connected with the supervision and direction of personnel and programs need to be aware of the legal implications of their actions. Many human service administrators come from the ranks of social workers and as such may have no formal training in these matters. They may learn about legal issues as the problems arise. This deficit could put both individuals and the agency at risk of liability.

EMPLOYMENT LAW

Federal and state laws govern personnel matters. The agency or practice group may choose to hire a social worker to work full or part time. The advantage of using employees is that the agency is fully in control of all aspects of the worker's performance and evaluation (Yenney and APA 1994). The disadvantage is that the employer must comply with state and federal laws regarding taxes, including Social Security and Medicare taxes, and payment into mandated employee benefit programs such as workers' compensation and unemployment insurance. These costs, in combination with the cost of employer-provided benefits, can add as much as 30 percent to the cost of the worker's base salary. Employers are required to file tax forms and maintain accurate records on all employees. The failure to pay taxes and make required contributions can result in criminal charges as well as exposure to the payment of back taxes, plus interest and potentially stiff fines.

Some agencies have sought to save money and increase flexibility by hiring professionals as independent contractors. The advantages of this arrangement include the money and time savings of not having to pay taxes and maintain detailed employment records on the worker. The obvious disadvantage is the independence of the worker in performing the agreed-upon assignments. Administrators are not able to exert control of the methods or activities of an independent contractor as they can those of an employee.

Agencies may require legal advice to determine whether a worker is an employee or an independent contractor. The legal test includes about twenty factors and is difficult to apply. If an agency hires someone as an independent contractor, but the Internal Revenue Service later determines the conditions of the work relationship actually meet the criteria for an employee, the agency would be liable for all unpaid taxes. If a prospective worker has a separate principal place of business, with evidence such as an office, business cards, letterhead, and other such materials, and the person is paid to perform a specific service, the argument for independent contractor status is stronger.

When an agency contracts with a worker, it takes on legal responsibilities beyond the filing of taxes and the maintenance of records. These legal issues begin in the hiring process, include supervisory and disciplinary systems, and continue into the termination of a worker from an agency. Employers should plan for the hiring of new staff by reviewing the agency's affirmative action plan. Most employers are governed by Title VII of the Civil Rights Act of 1964 as amended by the Equal Employment Opportunity Act of 1972. These regulations prohibit an agency from discriminating in the employment process on the basis of race, color, religion, national or ethnic origin, age, gender, physical handicap, or political beliefs.

The development of clear job descriptions, level of experience, and qualifications necessary for each position are important prerequisites for complying with legal mandates. First, the specific criteria allow for objective evaluation of candidates. Discrimination is a failure to treat all people equally, where no reasonable distinction exists between those favored and those not favored (*Black's* 1983). When an administrator or search committee rates candidates according to predetermined criteria, the employer reduces the possibility of discrimination in hiring. Any decision regarding hiring must be based on legitimate job-related criteria.

DISABILITY LAW

A second hiring issue requiring clear job descriptions involves candidates with disabilities. The Americans with Disabilities Act is an extraordinarily comprehensive statute that prohibits discrimination and provides legal protections for workers and job applicants who have a documented disability. Employers are not allowed to inquire about a person's disabling condition before making an offer of employment. The written job descriptions should specify the "essential functions" for each position. If a candidate with a disability can perform the essential functions, the employer has an obligation to make reasonable accommodations to meet the needs of the employee. For example, a social worker with severe arthritis may be unable to type on a computer. These skills are important for maintaining client records and correspondence, but the position's essential functions relate to effective counseling skills. The employer could allow the person to use a tape recorder or voice recognition system to maintain treatment records.

Determining whether an accommodation is reasonable and whether a candidate is a qualified individual is often difficult. Historically, most employers have not been willing to investigate options to enable a person with a disability to become employed. Social service agencies should attempt to recruit and retain workers with diverse backgrounds, including those with disabilities. To accomplish this goal effectively agencies must make an active and creative commitment to accommodate the needs of people with disabilities (Madden 1995).

This does not mean that an employer must accommodate in every situation. The analysis of whether the accommodation is reasonable is based on the relative burden that it puts on the employer. If the cost of the accommodation is unduly burdensome, as it relates to the size of the agency budget and the conditions of employment, the law may not require the agency to make the accommodation. If an agency determines that a disability prevents a candidate from meeting essential job functions, the statute does not require it to hire the disabled candidate. In all cases employers must not use myths about the disability as a basis for making a determination concerning a job applicant's qualifications. The Supreme Court has pared the scope of the ADA in recent years, but the act's applicability to those with major disabling conditions remains strong. Agency administrators should consult human resource professionals to remain current with this changing area of law.

TERMINATION OF EMPLOYEES

Terminating workers produces high emotions and may result in legal challenges. In many states the employment of a worker who does not have a written contract is "at will." Technically, this means that the employer does not have to give a reason for firing a worker (Epstein 1984). In practice, however, most professionals have some contractual protections by virtue of an employee handbook or some other "agreement" that specifies the rules of conduct for both employers and employees.

Even where a handbook does not exist, the courts may imply the conditions from the usual practices in the field. For this reason, every agency should have clear, written procedures covering employment issues, such as

- Grievance procedures to handle workers' complaints against supervisors
- Disciplinary procedures, including warning and suspension terms
- Termination procedures, including people responsible, time lines, and an appeals process

Each area should comply with basic due process protections for workers, which include adequate notice of the problem, an opportunity to be heard, and a structure for making the decision. If the agency receives public funding, the due process may be required as a constitutional issue, but even when the agency is private, due process guarantees provide excellent evidence to courts that a termination was handled fairly. If a worker challenges a termination on either contract or constitutional grounds, the defining issue is whether a clear and adequate process was in place and whether the employer followed the process.

LEGAL ISSUES IN THE BUSINESS OF
A PRIVATE PRACTICE

When Amanda received a promotion at her company, it meant that she and her husband, Roger, would have to move to a new city. The timing of the move was attractive to the couple. Roger, a clinical social worker, had been working for a community mental health clinic for seven years. He had recently begun to do some private practice, sharing office space with two colleagues. He liked the freedom and challenge of working for himself, so when Amanda's new job required them to move, Roger knew the time was right to open a private practice. Graduate school had been a great place to learn theory and to develop clinical skills. However, as he reflected on his training, Roger realized that he had no understanding of how to start or run his business. The real estate agent who sold the couple their new home offered to help Roger find office space in a good location. She also recommended that Roger seek help in establishing the business from the lawyer who would be handling the real estate closing.

Roger found that sitting in the office of the lawyer, Bob, was like being in a foreign country with vastly different cultural traditions. Roger listened as Bob talked about "other psychiatrists" he has as clients, and Bob told stories about how crazy some of his own clients were. Roger was uncomfortable with the conversation and secretly worried that he was paying more than a hundred dollars an hour to listen to the lawyer tell stories. When they got down to business, Bob suggested that Roger would want to incorporate his practice. Bob said that this would create a legal entity that would shield Roger personally from liability should one of his clients decide to sue. Roger was unaware of the various options that were available for structuring his new business. The protection of his personal assets, particularly his new home, was a major concern.

After getting some basic information, Bob assured Roger that he would file the necessary paperwork with the state to establish a professional corporation. Bob reviewed the requirements for maintaining corporate status and suggested that Roger meet with him in a few weeks to review the tax implications of the practice. Roger had a headache as he left the office. He wished that he had asked more questions but felt overwhelmed by the material.

Unfortunately, the legal issues in the business of social work are complex and difficult to master. The rules are subject to change as federal and state statutes and tax codes evolve. The concepts are foreign and uninteresting. Most practitioners are uncomfortable with the business end of their practice because it is different from the real work, which is providing help to clients. The natural conflict between altruism and materialism arises for many mental health practitioners when they have to make decisions involving legal issues such as billing, collections, caseload management, and dealing with insurance companies.

ESTABLISHING A PRACTICE

When social workers decide to start a private practice, most give extensive attention to the tasks of choosing office space and selecting a functional computer and software, as well as exploring advertising and marketing strategies to generate referrals. They rarely give adequate consideration to what form of business they will use. Like Roger in the example case, social workers turn to lawyers to advise them about the best strategy. However, if social workers march like lemmings into the turbulent seas of the business world without articulating their particular needs, the results will prove unsatisfying. Not every lawyer is an expert in setting up a mental health practice. The most appropriate form of business for a mental health practice depends on many factors, such as the type of services to be offered, the number and type of professionals involved, the plan for the future growth of the business, and the personal financial circumstances of the individuals. Each state has its own rules for establishing businesses, and social workers must examine these rules before making a final decision. However, the key issues for most social workers are liability and taxes.

The first task for those social workers thinking of opening a practice is to select a team of business advisers. Just as they would be reckless to treat a client by using a new technique without first obtaining training and supervision, social workers should make no business decisions without planning and advice from legal and financial experts. The professionals they should consult include a lawyer, accountant, insurance agent, and banker. Despite excellent skills and good intentions, every social worker assumes some risk when engaging in mental health practice. The business structure and financial plan enable the social worker to protect against risks while generating a reasonable income.

If a social worker does not elect to choose a particular form, the business usually will take the form of a sole proprietorship or partnership, depending on the number of individuals involved. This choice may or may not serve the interests of the social worker. In many cases mental health professionals elect to establish a more formal business structure than a sole proprietorship or partnership.

A corporation is a legal concept that the law regards as a separate entity from the individuals who are the principles in the business. Each of these forms—sole proprietorship, partnership, and corporation—has advantages and disadvantages. The prudent choice for each practitioner depends on a number of factors that need to be analyzed for each individual situation. Before I describe the various options, readers need to be familiar with several important legal and business terms and concepts.

LIMITED LIABILITY

The concept of limited liability refers to the risk exposure of a person who is operating a business. When business owners risk only their investment in and the assets of the business, they are said to have limited liability. Although corporations, chapter S corporations, limited liability corporations, and, to some extent, limited partnerships provide limited liability to the individual social worker, such limited liability is not absolute. For mental health workers, a prevailing concern is that a malpractice suit could outstrip insurance coverage, leaving the individual personally liable. This type of exposure could jeopardize the social worker's house or other personal/family assets. Although this situation is rare, it is a possibility.

Therefore, social workers are most concerned with setting up a business structure that protects against this scenario. What they often overlook is that liability may arise from several different sources. Businesses may incur liability by, for example, taking on a debt, such as when the business borrows money to purchase a building or office equipment or takes a lease out on a property. Liability also may come from the business's failure to perform the requirements of a contract. For these types of legal claims, a business structure that provides for limited liability does protect an individual's personal assets.

But these business structures may lose their limited liability protection or it may be extended in certain circumstances. Three common scenarios can result in the loss of limited liability: guarantees; negligent, reckless, or intentional conduct; or the "piercing of the corporate veil." Banks and office equipment suppliers may be willing to extend credit to new counseling practices, but they usually require the owners to either co-sign or guarantee the amount of the credit. If the practice defaults on a loan or fails to repay the credit, the individual who signed the loan guarantee becomes liable for the remaining balance. In effect, the act of guaranteeing a loan extends individual liability, despite the presence of a corporate entity.

Liability may also arise from the wrongful or negligent conduct of social workers or employees, including malpractice claims. In most states no corporate structure fully protects personal assets from malpractice claims or other intentional or negligent acts. Any person who intentionally or negligently harms another will be responsible and liable for any resulting injuries and damage. This is true regardless of whether the individual was acting for himself or the business. A social worker who commits malpractice cannot hide behind the business's limited liability to avoid personal responsibility. However, in the event that an employee, and not the individual owner–social worker, has committed the malpractice, the employee and the business entity may be liable, but the individual owner will retain the limited liability protection. Purchasing supplemental insurance may protect against certain risks. If practitioners can eliminate or reduce the exposure to personal liability at a relatively minor cost, they should consider doing so.

PASS-THROUGH TAX STATUS

Many human service professionals proudly admit to being naive about taxes. With its complicated rules and formulas, the tax code is better left to the accountants. However, the different business structures have important tax implications. Because a corporation is a separate entity, the earnings of the corporation are subject to federal taxes and, usually, those required by the state where the corporation does business. Wages that the corporation pays to a social worker are taxed at the individual tax rate. In effect, the income from the practice is taxed twice. In some business structures such as partnerships, the tax code allows for pass-through tax status. The advantage of pass-through tax status is that it avoids double taxation. The earnings of the business pass through to the owner, who pays only individual income taxes. In the case of multiple owners the income is divided according to the agreement of the parties and the earnings pass through to them.

In most states several different legal forms are available to the social worker, including the sole proprietorship, partnership, corporation, and a limited liability corporation (often referred to as an LLC). Several of these structures have a number of varieties, but a description of these exceeds the scope of this chapter and would unnecessarily complicate the discussion.

SOLE PROPRIETORSHIP

A sole proprietorship is the simplest legal form that a business can take. It involves one individual, who owns the entire business and makes a profit. It requires few formalities and carries with it the most risk to the individual because liability is unlimited. The law considers the practice's assets and liabilities to be the same as the individual's assets and liabilities (Stromberg et al. 1988). If the practice incurs a debt or obligation, such as a judgment from a malpractice suit, the individual's assets are accessible to the creditors. Practitioners should be aware of this because juries often award damages in excess of the limits of a professional liability insurance policy. Also, if the lawsuit was for activities outside the coverage of the policy (such as sexual misconduct with a client), the policy may not cover the losses at all. Another disadvantage to a sole proprietorship is that it lacks continuity because it ends upon the death of the owner. It is not an asset that can be sold or otherwise transferred.

The sole proprietor is responsible for paying self-employment taxes to cover Social Security and unemployment. Many social workers new to private practice are unaware that estimated payments are due every quarter throughout the year. Failure to make appropriate tax payments is a violation of the law and could result in substantial fines against the social worker.

The main benefit to choosing to structure a practice as a sole proprietorship is its simplicity. For those who are uncomfortable with the business side of practice, this structure has the fewest initial and ongoing requirements. One merely needs to hang up the proverbial shingle, open the doors, serve the clients, report the income, and pay the taxes. But mental health professionals must consider whether this simplicity is worth the liability risks and whether a more formal organizational structure would better address the long-term needs of the individual and the practice.

GROUP PRACTICE OPTIONS

Many mental health practitioners enter private practice by affiliating with an existing practice. Often the social worker has limited understanding of the structure of the group or of the legal relationships that joining the practice creates. Group practice can have legal and clinical benefits, including the opportunity to rely on colleagues for consultation and for coverage of one's caseload, the opportunity to benefit from established referral streams, and the existence of standardized systems for practice evaluation, client billing, insurance tracking, and other clinical record keeping. At the same time, involvement in a group practice may lead to increased liability, depending on the type of business organization, the quality of the professionals in the group, and the type of population/problem that each professional in the group deals with.

PARTNERSHIPS. A partnership is a legal entity much like a sole proprietorship in its simplicity and vulnerability, except that it involves two or more owners who come together to make a profit. Every state (with the exception of Louisiana) has adopted the Uniform Partnership Act, which governs the structure and function of partnerships. It is important to obtain the help of a lawyer who is experienced in drafting partnership agreements. Social workers who are contemplating this business organization should make certain that the partnership agreement is in writing and covers all eventualities. For example, each partner may contribute a different percentage to the expenses of the practice and would receive a predetermined amount or percentage of income. The partnership agreement also should specify those situations that will result in dissolution of the partnership. In most cases, if a partner leaves the practice, the remaining partners would have to dissolve the partnership and re-form it. Note that the partnership is not completely terminated until all the activities of the business are finalized. As I noted earlier, the partnership itself is not taxed. All profits and losses pass through to the individual partners, according to their share in the partnership.

If one partner is found to be liable for a damage award, debt, or other liability as a result of an action within the scope of the ordinary duties of the partnership, all partners share the liability equally. The law in most states is that each member of the partnership is "jointly and severally" liable for the debt. This means that a creditor could sue one or all partners for the full amount. An individual partner, forced to pay a partner's debt completely, might subsequently be able to recoup payments from the other partners. This is why it is important to choose partners carefully and to monitor the professionalism and practice of all members. A court can infer that a partnership exists when a practice group acts as if it is a partnership. This might occur in relation to a lawsuit against one member of a practice group that does not have any formal agreement but informally shares office space, supplies, and billing services. Courts will examine the relationship and may impose liability on the other members of a group practice for the transgressions of one social worker if the court finds evidence of an intent to share in the profits or otherwise establish the practice as a joint enterprise.

CORPORATIONS. A corporation is a more formal business structure than either a sole proprietorship or a partnership. In the eyes of the law a corporation is an independent legal entity, separate and apart from the individual owner(s). People who have an ownership interest in the corporation are called shareholders. The corporate structure offers more protection to the business owners in the form of limited liability but requires more formalities. For example, each corporation must elect officers, conduct regular shareholder meetings, and maintain specific records concerning the financial activities of the business. All shareholders must have access to these records.

Since a corporation is a separate entity, it is taxed as a separate entity. In addition, corporations have different tax rates than individuals. It is often said that a characteristic of a corporation is "double taxation" in that the corporate profits, after being taxed at the corporate tax rate, are then taxed again when such profits are distributed to the individual owners (shareholders) in the form of dividends. However, a corporation that has a well-thought-out business plan can avoid paying taxes on most of the corporate proceeds by paying dividends to its members in the same year that the corporation earns the income, because the result is negligible corporate income. One advantage to the corporate business structure is the tax benefits that it receives from buying health and retirement benefits for its officers, employees, and shareholders. Because the corporation makes these payments as part of the overhead of the practice, they are a pretax expense. In a sole proprietorship the income accrues directly to the individual, who would have to pay for the benefits with this income.

A corporation can assume a number of different forms. The two most important ones for mental health professionals are the professional corporation and the limited liability corporation. Each state has its own regulations on corporations, so any decision about choice of form needs to consider the specific statutes.

Professional service corporations (PCs) allow individuals who share a particular professional license to form a business. In most states only those individuals who are licensed for the same service may be members or shareholders in the professional corporation. In other words, a professional service corporation established by a group of psychologists to offer psychological services would have to limit the ownership of the business to psychologists licensed in the state in which the business is incorporated. Unlike a general corporation, a shareholder of a PC may not transfer ownership to another person who is not similarly licensed. However, shareholders are allowed to assign their income from the business to an unlicensed individual.

A limited liability corporation is the newest form for a small business and is particularly well suited for a mental health practice. An LLC combines the limited liability advantages of the corporation with the ease of management and the pass-through tax status of a partnership. Relatively unknown just a few years ago, the LLC is available to residents of most states in some form. Changes in the federal tax code that went into effect in 1997 eliminated some of the complicated rules that formerly regulated this area. Currently, LLCs are so easy to establish that one expert commented that his Labrador retriever could set one up (Fleming 1997). The LLC is made up of two or more shareholders who are protected by limited liability but taxed as a partnership. The owners of a limited liability company are liable only for their initial investment in the company.

A limited liability company is easy both to form and manage; the management requirements are much simpler than those for a corporation. The principles need not hold directors' or shareholders' meetings and therefore need not keep minutes. Instead of a complicated set of bylaws, the limited liability company can be run according to the terms of a simple set of regulations or an operating agreement. The law places no restrictions on who can be an owner of a limited liability company. The LLC is flexible and can be managed informally, like a partnership, with all owners having equal say in its management. As in a partnership, the sale of an ownership interest, death of an owner, bankruptcy of an owner, or other similar event results in the dissolution of the company and the termination of the business (absent an agreement to the contrary).

Many social workers make business decisions solely on the advice of an attorney. If the lawyer happens to be experienced in establishing small businesses, knows something about mental health practice, and is sensitive to the individual financial situation of the practitioner, the advice is likely to be beneficial. Social workers can increase the chances that they will make a wise choice about the structure of the business by being knowledgeable consumers of business advice. When deciding on the form of the practice, social workers must consider with whom they are going into business and whether their interests are compatible. They must be forward thinking in considering what future endeavors the business might undertake and what business structure will best accommodate these developments. Social workers must weigh the need for liability protection and tax advantages against the desire to have a structure that is simple to set up and to maintain. Social workers must understand the concept of limited liability and realize that in most states the liability for malpractice runs to the personal assets of the individual social worker. The personal protection afforded by the various corporate forms is for debts and obligations of the business and the intentional or negligent acts of others in the practice. Once social workers clearly understand this concept, they will find that whether they need to incorporate becomes an easier decision to make.

APPENDIX: LEGAL RESEARCH

L AW IS A DISCIPLINE that is never settled. Information affecting the status of laws emerges daily from legal cases in local, state, and federal courts across the nation. Legislatures pass new laws and amend existing ones. Administrative agencies promulgate regulations that interpret and apply statutes in ways that often differ from the views of previous administrations. Legal scholars develop theoretical models that influence the direction of particular areas of the law. How does a social worker keep up with a landscape that is always changing?

It is helpful to remember that the law is a set of rules given form by court decisions and administrative regulations. Social workers seek legal information to understand how the legal system would rule in a given circumstance or, more often, to seek guidance regarding what they need to do to comply with the law. Some legal research guides place too much emphasis on the formal legal research strategies that lawyers use. A novice can find legal research overwhelming. Luckily, most circumstances do not require advanced legal research. The place to start is by understanding the purpose of your legal research and by developing skills for locating essential information.

STATUTORY LAW

In every area of practice social workers must be familiar with statutes that directly influence the practice environment and the therapeutic relationship, as well as common legal issues faced by the client population. For example, does your state have a law that allows adolescents to have counseling without parental consent? If so, is it limited to certain issues such as suicide, substance abuse, or AIDS counseling and testing? Is the right to consent to treatment limited by age (for example, only those mature minors older than sixteen)? What does the law say about the effect of a restraining order on visitation in a custody case? What are the rights of a tenant who is being evicted from an apartment? Social workers must know how to find the relevant statutes in order to be familiar with the legal requirements that affect their practice and the rights and interests of their clients.

Fortunately, legal research of state and federal statutes has become much easier with the introduction of electronic databases for each state. Many of these sites maintain search engines to assist in the retrieval of a statute. Most state legal codes are organized by subject. The key to locating the law that you are looking for is to understand how the law may be classified in the system of statutes. Begin by thinking about what words or phrases describe the class of situations (Kunz et al. 2000). In legal research this is sometimes referred to as issue spotting. The process starts with a review of the facts to frame the legal question in correct terms. Is it a tort or a contract issue? For example, in looking up a statute on privileged communication, you might be tempted to look in the section on licensing or a more general section on social service law. However, most privilege statutes appear in the evidence section, because privilege is an exception to the rule that requires people to provide evidence to a court or administrative hearing.

You should use annotated versions of state and federal statutes to locate related case law. The annotations note those cases that interpret or otherwise rule on each section of the statute. It is then easy to read the case to develop a more thorough understanding of the scope and reach of a particular statute. These annotated versions of the statutes are generally not available in free, online searches, but they are available in legal libraries. Legal treatises and encyclopedias also provide an effective starting point for legal research on statutes. For example, if you wish to research Social Security law, a search of *American Law Reports* or a legal encyclopedia would define terms, provide the citations to relevant law, and discuss important cases in this area of the law.

CASE LAW

One problem with legal research involves the development of the research question. In many cases the question is too specific for effective legal research. The legal reasoning section of this book discusses the need to broaden a legal issue to its critical elements. It is easy to get frustrated. Use a legal dictionary to understand the legal concepts, and use the broader terms to search for cases.

For example, a social worker in a community mental health center is assigned to a client who is has a chronic mental illness that responds well to a stable environment. As a result of a bureaucratic mistake by your agency and the state mental health department, the client was removed from the Medicaid managed-care program. This type of mistake has occurred with increasing frequency since the state changed computer systems. The complaints of the workers have been met with threats that troublemakers will be fired. When the client attempted to get his prescriptions refilled, he was told he needed to pay in cash. The client panicked and did not return to his supervised apartment. He subsequently suffered increased paranoid symptoms and was found one week later with injuries from a severe beating. As his caseworker, you feel that he has suffered an unnecessary injury directly as a result of the actions of your agency. How would you define the issue? Does your client have a right to sue? What job protection would you have if you blew the whistle on the administration? Could you file an administrative complaint? What agency might have jurisdiction?

Searching with key words such as *whistle-blower, managed care*, and *negligence* or *mental health law* provides the worker with useful information. Once you have an understanding of the key terms, a search of the local state laws and cases is more productive. Social workers are unable to make effective decisions about a course of action in a case such as this without a foundation in basic legal research.

In legal research locating one good case makes the remaining research significantly easier and more productive. Two legal research companies have developed index systems to ease the process of finding related cases and checking on the status of a case. Starting with the case citation, it is possible to locate all published decisions that have cited that case or discussed that issue by using Shepards (LexisNexis) or Key Cite (Westlaw). These services, available in both print and on-line formats, use citations and indexes to categorize legal issues and link cases that discuss the same legal issues. Shepards citations list all the cases that have discussed the case, which makes it possible to use the citations to read similar cases, including those from your jurisdiction. In this way, you will find the leading cases and legal issues. Westlaw's Key Cite system uses headnotes (coded summaries of discrete legal issues discussed in the case) to classify the legal issues in each case. The service assigns key numbers to these legal issues, and researchers can use the numbers to find cases that have dealt with the same issue.

Reviewing legal cases calls for two key strategies. First, taking notes is a tremendous aid to following and remembering the reasoning of complex cases (Wren and Wren 1986). Second, once you have researched the issue, it is important to regularly update the research (Jacobstein, Mersky, and Dunn 1994). Legal decisions can change over time, and a case that seemed important subsequently may be overruled or clarified.

Some articles in social work journals analyze legal trends and discuss important legal decisions. For example, Kopels and Sheridan have written about the legal status of child custody for women in domestic violence situations (2002), and Madden and Parody have written about legal issues in recovered memory cases (1997). The analysis of legal issues and trends from a social work perspective provides information that social workers need for working for legal reforms and for adjusting their practice policies to meet emerging trends in the law. To date, this area of social work scholarship has been insufficiently developed.

ELECTRONIC LEGAL RESEARCH

As I mentioned, the world of electronic research has simplified the task of legal research. It is not complicated to conduct a search for cases or materials using the Lexis database or to retrieve the text of a statute from a state website. Law.com, for example, provides legal resources, information, and articles. A number of libraries, such as Cornell Law School's, organize legal material and support basic legal research. The electronic law sites have become more thorough, easier to navigate, and more intuitive for users. A list and brief description of some of the prominent sites, as well as links to these sites, appear on the website for this book.

The following electronic law sites are free and contain good starting points for researching general legal concepts and for linking to specific legal information. Several sites require free registration, and others have advanced services and sections available to paying subscribers only.

- Discussion lists at Behavior OnLine <www.behavior.net>, especially "Law, Ethics, and Psychotherapy," moderated by William Reid. This discussion list deals with common legal and ethical issues in practice. Dr. Reid, a psychiatrist with an extensive background in the law, responds to situations described by and questions from psychotherapists.
- Center for Law and Social Policy <www.clasp.org>. The Center for Law and Social Policy (CLASP), a national nonprofit organization founded in 1968,

conducts research and policy analysis and offers technical assistance and advocacy on issues related to economic security for low-income families with children. The site has articles and information related to social welfare laws.

- Information about federal courts <www.uscourts.gov/UFC99.pdf>. This is a government document (PDF file) that explains the federal court system and provides useful information about the jurisdictions and roles of the various courts.
- FindLaw <www.findlaw.com>. This is an excellent starting point for on-line legal research. This site contains a vast collection of legal materials, links to state materials, and articles and essays on legal subjects.
- U.S. Constitution <http://conlaw.usatoday.findlaw.com/constitution/index.html>. This *USA Today* site provides a copy of the Constitution, constitutional amendments, and a collection of some annotations of important cases.
- Psychiatry and Law Updates <www.reidpsychiatry.com>. This is William Reid's website. It contains good analyses of legal issues in clinical mental health practice and summaries of recent case law.
- John Hopkins Law Library on-line guide <www.library.jhu.edu/gpml/find-it/legalresources/legalbasics.html>. This site offers explanations of basic legal research topics, including legal citation, abbreviations, an on-line legal dictionary, and search strategies.
- Jurist: The Law School Source <http://jurist.law.pitt.edu/dictionary.htm>. This site contains a browsable dictionary of legal terminology and legal procedure.
- Internet Law Library <www.lawguru.com/ilawlib/index.html>. This site houses a vast collection of federal, state, and international statutes and treaties and searchable databases. The site is hosted by lawguru.com, a site that sells standard legal forms and self-help legal materials.
- Legal Information Institute, Cornell Law School <www.law.cornell.edu>. This is an extensive collection of materials on constitutional issues. Visit the topical libraries to learn about the parameters and issues on a variety of legal topics.
- LexisONE, a state law resource center <www.lexisone.com/legalresearch/legalguide/states/states_resources_index.htm>. Links to the state pages contain state statutes, legislative websites, state offices, rules of court, administrative regulations, and so on. This page is a one-stop website for locating a broad variety of legal information from each state.
- Mediation Library <http://www.mediate.com/articles>. This website contains a number of articles on mediation practice that are useful to social workers who wish to know more about this field.

- Nolo Law Center <www.nolo.com/index.cfm>. This site provides a variety of legal research resources—legal news and developments and "plain English" law centers on a variety of topics of interest to social workers. It also offers standard legal forms and materials for sale.
- National College of Probate Judges Links <www.ncpj.org/links.html>. This site has links to state sites detailing cases, analyzing probate issues, and providing background information on the probate court process.
- The National Center for Social Gerontology <www.tcsg.org/lslinks.htm>. State-by-state links to legal service providers for older Americans.
- The Federal Web Locator <www.infoctr.edu/fwl>. This service, provided by the Center for Information Law and Policy, is intended to be the one-stop-shopping point for on-line information about the federal government.
- Directory of Lawyer Disciplinary Agencies <www.abanet.org/cpr/disciplinary.html>. This American Bar Association site has links to the organization in each jurisdiction that handles complaints against lawyers. The site also has links to information about legal ethics and standards of conduct.
- Civil Rights Project, Harvard Law School <www.law.harvard.edu/groups/civilrights>. The Civil Rights Project is a leading organization devoted to civil rights research. It has found eager collaborators among researchers nationwide and wide open doors among advocacy organizations, policy makers, and journalists.

The two premier subscription services for electronic legal research are LexisNexis and Westlaw. Individual or agency subscriptions are expensive, and charges are calculated based on the amount of time spent on line. Many libraries subscribe to LexisNexis and provide free access to this service, both its legal and general research capabilities.

REFERENCES

Albert, R. 2000. *Law and social work practice.* 2d ed. New York: Springer.

American Bar Association. 1999. *Model rules of professional conduct.* Washington, D.C.: American Bar Association.

American Bar Association Commission on Legal Problems of the Elderly. 2000. *Building coalitions in aging, disability, and dispute resolution.* http://www.mediate.com/articles/aba1.cfm. (December 4, 2002).

American Law Institute. 2001. Principles of the law of family dissolution: Analysis and recommendations. *Duke Journal of Gender Law and Policy* 8:1–60.

Amsterdam, A. G. and J. S. Bruner. 2000. *Minding the law.* New York: Harvard Press.

Andrews, A. B. 1990. Interdisciplinary and interorganizational collaboration. In A. Manahan, ed., *Encyclopedia of social work,* 18th ed., 1990 supp., pp. 175–88. Washington, D.C.: NASW Press.

Aquinas, Thomas. [1266–72] 1945. Concerning the nature of law. In *Summa theologica: The basic writings of Saint Thomas Aquinas.* Vol. 2. Edited by A. Pegis. New York: Random House.

Austin, John. 1873. *The province of jurisprudence determined.* In *The province of jurisprudence etc.* Reprint; 1954. London: Weidenfeld and Nicolson.

Barker, R. L. 1995. *The social work dictionary.* 3d ed. Washington, D.C.: NASW Press.

Barker, R. L. and D. M. Branson. 2000. *Forensic social work: Legal aspects of professional practice.* 2d ed. New York: Haworth Press.

Barnhizer, D. 2000. Princes of darkness and angels of light: The soul of the American lawyer. *Notre Dame Journal of Law, Ethics, and Public Policy* 14:371–477.

Berlin, S. B. and J. C. Marsh. 1993. *Informing practice decisions.* New York: Macmillan.

Berns, S. 1993. *Concise jurisprudence.* Sidney, Australia: Federation Press.

Black's law dictionary. 1983. 5th ed. St. Paul, Minn.: West.

Briar-Lawson, K. and J. Drews. 2000. Child and family welfare policies and services: Current issues and historical antecedents. In J. Midgley, M. B. Tracy, and M. Livermore, eds., *The Handbook of Social Policy*, pp. 157–71. Thousand Oaks, Calif.: Sage.

Brooks, P. and P. Gerwitz, eds. 1996. *Law's stories: Narrative and rhetoric in the law.* New Haven, Conn.: Yale University Press.

Brooks, S. L. 1999. Therapeutic jurisprudence and preventive law in child welfare proceedings: A family systems approach. *Psychology, Public Policy, and Law* 5:951–65.

———. 2000. Therapeutic and preventive approaches to school safety: Applications of a family systems model. *New England Law Review* 34:615–22.

Buckley, W. R. 1993. *Torts and personal injury law.* Albany, N.Y.: Delmar.

Cardozo, B. N. 1921. *The nature of the judicial process.* New Haven, Conn.: Yale University Press.

Cohen, J. R. 1999. Advising clients to apologize. *Southern California Law Review* 72:1009–69.

Congress, E. P. 1999. *Social work values and ethics.* Chicago: Nelson-Hall.

Council on Social Work Education. 1998. *Working paper on interprofessional education principles.* Alexandria, Va.: Council on Social Work Education.

Crump, D. and J. B. Berman. 1985. *The story of a civil suit:* Dominguez v. Scott's Food Stores. Houston, Tex.: John Marshall Publishing.

Daicoff, S. 1997. Lawyer, know thyself: A review of empirical research on attorney attributes bearing on professionalism. *American University Law Review* 46:1337–1427.

Dernbach, J. C. and R. V. Singleton. 1981. *A practical guide to legal writing and legal method.* Littleton, Colo.: Rothman.

Dickson, D. T. 1998. *Confidentiality and privacy in social work: A guide to the law for practitioners and students.* New York: Free Press.

Diller, M. 2000. The new localism in welfare advocacy. *St. Louis University Public Law Review* 19:413–28.

Dworkin, R. 1986. *Laws empire.* Cambridge, Mass.: Harvard University Press.

———. 1996. *Freedom's law: The moral reading of the American Constitution.* Cambridge, Mass.: Harvard University Press.

Ehrlich, S. A. 2000. The increasing federalization of crime. *Arizona State Law Journal* 32:825–42.

Eisemann, V. H. 2001. Striking a balance of fairness: Sexual orientation and voir dire. *Yale Journal of Law and Feminism* 13:1–27.

Epstein, R. A. 1984. In defense of the contract at will. *University of Chicago Law Review* 51:947–82.

— 1985. *Simple rules for a complex world.* Cambridge, Mass.: Harvard University Press.

Faller, K. C. 1998. Parental alienation syndrome: What is it and what data support it? *Child Maltreatment* 3:100–15.

Feinman, J. M. 2000. *Law 101*. New York: Oxford University Press.

Fleming, C. E. 1997. LLCs are easier to set up. *Lawyers Weekly USA* 97, no. 1 (January 13): 1, 12.

Flynn, C. P. 1993. The New Jersey antistalking laws: Putting an end to a "fatal attraction." *Seton Hall Legislative Journal* 18:297–330.

Gaetke, E. R. 1998. Litigating zealously within the bounds of the law: Forward: Renewed introspection and the legal profession. *Kentucky Law Journal* 87:903–18.

Gaskins, R. 1981. The role of discretion in the legal and social service systems. *Social Casework* 62:387–97.

Gifford, E. P. 1995. 42 U.S.C. 1983 and Social Worker Immunity: A Cause of Action Denied. *Texas Tech Law Review* 26:1013–38.

Goldkamp, J. S. 2000. The drug court response: Issues and implications for justice change. *Albany Law Review* 63:923–61.

Goldstein, J., Anna Freud, and A. Solnit. 1973. *Beyond the best interest of the children*. New York: Free Press.

Greenawalt, K. 1992. *Law and objectivity*. New York: Oxford University Press.

Hafemeister, T. L. 1999. End-of-life decision making, therapeutic jurisprudence, and preventive law: Hierarchical versus consensus-based decision-making model. *Arizona Law Review* 41:329–73.

Hanna, F. J., W. B. Talley, and M. H. Guindon. 2000. The power of perception: Toward a model of cultural oppression and liberation. *Journal of Counseling and Development* 78:430–41.

Harris, D. A. 1999. Driving while black: Racial profiling on our nation's highways. *American Civil Liberties Union Special Report*. Washington, D.C.: American Civil Liberties Union.

Hart, H. L. A. 1983. 1776–1976: Law in the perspective of philosophy. In H. L. A. Hart, ed., *Essays in jurisprudence and philosophy*, pp. 145–58. New York: Oxford University Press.

Hazard, G. C. 1999. Sumner Canary Lecture: Under shelter of confidentiality. *Case Western Reserve Law Review* 50:1–18.

Higuchi, S. and J. Coscia. 1995. Provider contracting issues are central to legal agenda. *American Psychological Association, Practitioner Focus*. http://www.apa.org/practice/pf/aug/95/contract.html. (December 4, 2002).

Hillman, R. A. 1997. *The richness of contract law: An analysis and critique of contemporary theories of contract law*. Boston: Kluwer Academic.

Houston-Vega, M. K., E. M. Nuehring, and E. R. Daguio. 1997. *Prudent practice: A guide for managing malpractice risk*. Washington, D.C.: NASW Press.

Jacobstein, J. M., R. M. Mersky, and D. J. Dunn. 1994. Legal research illustrated. 6th ed.. Westbury, N.Y.: Foundation Press.

Jansson, B. S. 1994. *Social policy: From theory to policy practice* 2d ed. Pacific Grove, Calif.: Brooks/Cole.

———. 1997. *The reluctant welfare state.* 3d ed.. Pacific Grove, Calif.: Brooks/Cole.

Johnson, J. R. 2000. Building multidisciplinary professional partnerships with the court on behalf of high-conflict divorcing families and their children: Who needs what kind of help? *University of Arkansas at Little Rock Law Review* 22:453–79.

Justice Policy Institute. 1999. *Second Chances: One Hundred Years of the Children's Court: Giving Kids a Chance to Make a Better Choice.* Washington, D.C.: Justice Policy Institute.

Kaplan, J. and J. R. Waltz. 1987. *Cases and materials on evidence.* 6th ed. Mineola, N.Y.: Foundation Press.

Kapp, M. B. 1996. Enhancing autonomy and choice in selecting and directing long-term care services. *Elder Law Journal* 4:55–97.

Kennedy, A. M. 1990. The constitution and the spirit of freedom, In *The Gauer Distinguished Lecture in Law and Public Policy,* 1:1–24. Washington, D.C.: National Legal Center for the Public Interest.

Klinck, R. A. 2001. Symposium: Reforming punitive damages: The punitive damage debate. *Harvard Journal on Legislation* 38:469–85.

Kopels, S. and M. C. Sheridan. 2002. Adding legal insult to injury: Battered women, their children, and the failure to protect. *Affilia* 17:9–29.

Kronman, A. 1998. Forward to A. L. Liman, *Lawyer: A life of counsel and controversy.* New York: Public Affairs.

Kunz, C. L., D. A. Schmedemann, M. P. Downs, and A. L. Bateson. 2000. *The process of legal research.* 5th ed.. New York: Aspen Law and Business.

Kurlychek, M., P. Torbet, and M. Bozynski. 1999. Focus on accountability: Best practices for juvenile court and probation. *JAIBG Bulletin,* August, pp. 1–14.

LaFave, W. R. 1988. *Modern criminal law.* 2d ed.. St. Paul, Minn.: West.

Landes, W. M. and R. A. Posner. 1987. *The economic structure of tort law.* Cambridge Mass.: Harvard University Press.

Langdell, C. C. 1871. *A selection of cases on the law of contracts.* Boston: Little, Brown.

Lens, V. 2001. The Supreme Court, federalism, and social policy: The new judicial activism. *Social Science Review* 75:318–36.

Levi, E. 1949. *An introduction to legal reasoning.* Chicago: University of Chicago Press.

Lipsky, M. 1987. Street-level bureaucrats as policy makers. In D. L. Yarwood, ed., *Public administration: Politics and the people,* pp. 121–38. New York: Longman.

Louisell, D. W., G. G. Hazard, and C. C. Tait. 1983. *Pleadings and procedure: State and federal.* 5th ed. Mineola, N.Y.: Foundation Press.

Madden, R. G. 1995. Disability law and undergraduate social work education: Practicing what we preach. *Journal of Baccalaureate Social Work* 1:71–83.

———. 1998. *Legal issues in social work, counseling, and mental health: Guidelines for clinical practice in psychotherapy.* Thousand Oaks, Calif.: Sage.

———. 2000a. Legal content in social work education: Preparing students for interprofessional practice. *Journal of Teaching in Social Work* 20(1–2): 3–16.

———. 2000b. *Legal Issues for Practice.* In P. Allen-Meares and C. Garvin, eds., *The Handbook of Social Work Direct Practice.* Thousand Oaks, Calif.: Sage.

Madden, R. G. and M. Parody. 1997. Between a legal rock and a practice hard place: Legal issues in recovered memory cases. *Clinical Social Work Journal* 25:223–47.

Madden, R. G. and R. Wayne. In press. Social work and the law: A therapeutic jurisprudence perspective. *Social Work.*

Maroney, R. M. 1991. *Social policy and social work: Critical essays on the welfare state.* New York: Aldine de Gruyter.

McKinnon, C. A. 1996. Law stories as reality and politics. In P. Brooks and P. Gerwitz, eds., *Law's stories: Narrative and rhetoric in the law,* pp. 232–37. New Haven, Conn.: Yale University Press.

McNeal, H. H. 2001. Unbundling and law school clinics: Where is the pedagogy? *Clinical Law Review* 7:341–402.

Meares, P. A. 1998. The interdisciplinary movement. *Journal of Social Work Education* 34(1): 2–5.

Moore, K. A., S. Vandivere, and J. Ehrle. 2000. Turbulence and child well-being. *National Survey of America's Families.* Series B. No. B-16. Washington, D.C.: Urban Institute.

Morgan, T. D. and R. D. Rotunda. 1988. *Selected standards on professional responsibility.* Mineola, N.Y.: Foundation Press.

Mosher, F. C. 1987. The professional state. In D. L. Yarwood, ed., *Public administration: Politics and the people,* pp. 187–98. New York: Longman.

Mounts, S. 1999. Malice aforethought in California: A history of legislative abdication and judicial vacillation. *University of San Francisco Law Review* 33:313–77.

Murphy, J. G. and J. L. Coleman. 1990. *Philosophy of law: An introduction to jurisprudence.* Rev. ed.. Boulder, Colo.: Westview.

National Association of Social Workers. 1990. *Standards for social work personnel practices.* Silver Spring, Md.: NASW.

———. 1999. *Code of Ethics.* Washington, D.C.: NASW.

National Center for State Courts. 1999. *National probate court standards.* Williamsburg, Va.: National Center for State Courts.

Nelson, D. W. 2000. ADR in the twenty-first century: Opportunities and challenges. *Dispute Resolution Magazine* 6(3): 3–5.

Nurse, A. R. and P. Thompson. 1999. Collaborative divorce: A new, interdisciplinary approach. *American Journal of Family Law* 13:226–34.

Patry, M. W., D. B. Wexler, D. P. Stolle, and A. J. Tomkins. 1998. Better legal counseling through empirical research: Identifying psycholegal soft spots and strategies. *California Western Law Review* 34:439–55.

Perlin, M. L. 1996. The voluntary delivery of mental health services in the community. In B. D. Sales and D. W. Shuman, eds., *Law, mental health, and mental disorder*, pp. 150–77. Pacific Grove, Calif.: Brooks/Cole.

Pettit, C. J. 2001. Vultures and lambs: A journey through protective services for the Texas elderly. *St. Mary's Law Journal* 33:57–99.

Plapinger, E. and D. Stienstra 1996. *ADR and settlement in the federal district courts: A sourcebook for judges and lawyers.* Federal Judicial Center. http://www.fjc.gov/public/pdf.nsf/lookup/adrsrcbk.pdf/$File/adrsrcbk.pdf (December 4, 2002).

Porsdam, H. 1999. *Legally speaking: Contemporary American culture and the law.* Amherst: University of Massachusetts Press.

Posner, R. A. 1990. *The problems of jurisprudence.* Cambridge, Mass.: Harvard University Press.

———. 1992. *Economic analysis of law.* 4th ed. Boston: Little, Brown.

———. 1996. *Law and legal theory in England and America.* Oxford: Oxford University Press.

———. 1999. The decline of formality in contract law. In F. H. Buckley, ed., *The fall and rise of freedom of contract,* pp. 61–78. Durham, N.C.: Duke University Press.

Pound, Roscoe. 1911. The scope and purpose of sociological jurisprudence. *Harvard Law Review* 24:591–619.

Preston-Shoot, M. 1997. Mapping social work: Definition, developments, and dialogue, *Liverpool Law Review* 20:115–17.

Price, M. O., H. Bitner, and S. R. Bysiewicz. 1979. *Effective legal research,* 4th ed. Boston: Little, Brown.

Quinn, M. C. 2000–2001. Whose team am I on anyway? Musings of a public defender about drug treatment court practice. *New York University Review of Law and Social Change* 26:37–75.

Rachlinski, J. R. 2000. The "new" law and psychology: A reply to critics, skeptics, and cautious supporters. *Cornell Law Review* 85:101–26.

Read, W. 1986. *Legal thinking: Its limits and tensions.* Philadelphia: University of Pennsylvania Press.

Restatement (Second) of Torts. 1965. Washington, D.C.: American Law Institute.

Riskin, L. L. and J. E. Westbrook. 1998. *Dispute resolution and lawyers.* Abridged 2d ed. St. Paul, Minn.: West.

Rosenberg, D. 1995. *The hidden Holmes: His theory of torts in history.* Cambridge, Mass.: Harvard University Press.

Rosenberg, J. A. 2000. Adapting unitary principles of professional responsibility to unique practice contexts: A reflective model for resolving ethical dilemmas in elder law. *Loyola University Chicago Law Journal* 31:405–84.

Rosenfeld, E. A. 2001. Mental health advance directives: A false sense of autonomy for the nation's aging population. *Elder Law Journal* 9:53–81.

Sales, B. D. and D. W. Shuman. 1996. The newly emerging mental health law. In B. D. Sales and D. W. Shuman, eds., *Law, mental health, and mental disorder,* pp. 2–14. Pacific Grove, Calif.: Brooks/Cole.

Saltzman, A. and K. Proch. 1990. *Law in social work practice.* Chicago: Nelson-Hall.

Samar, V. J. 1998. *Justifying judgment: Practicing law and philosophy.* Lawrence: University Press of Kansas.

Schepard, A. 2001. Editorial notes: Alienated children in divorce. *Family Court Review* 39:243–45.

Schma, W. G. 1997. Review of David B. Wexler and B. J. Winick, eds., *Law in a therapeutic key: Developments in therapeutic jurisprudence. Judges' Journal* 36(3): 81–82.

Schneider, R. L. and L. Lester. 2001. *Social work advocacy.* Belmont, Calif.: Brooks/Cole.

Schrager, S. 1999. *The trial lawyer's art.* Philadelphia: Temple University Press.

Schultz, D. T. 2000. Defending suicide-related malpractice cases: A lawyer's perspective. *Journal of Psychiatric Practice* 6:345–48.

Scott, E. S. and T. Grisso. 1997. The evolution of adolescence: A developmental perspective on juvenile justice reform. *Journal of Criminal Law and Criminology* 88:145–49.

Shapiro, J. 1995. The downside of managed mental health care. *Clinical Social Work Journal* 23:441–51.

Shapo, M. S. 1999. *Basic principles of tort law.* St. Paul, Minn.: West.

Sheafor, B. W., C. R. Horejsi, and G. A. Horejsi. 1991. *Techniques and guidelines for social work practice.* 2d ed. Boston: Allyn and Bacon.

Slawson, W. D. 1996. *Binding promises: The late twentieth-century reformation of contract law.* Princeton, N.J.: Princeton University Press.

Smith, C. E. 1991. *Courts and the poor.* Chicago: Nelson-Hall.

Spadaro, J. A. 1998. An elusive search for the truth: The admissibility of repressed and recovered memories in light of *Daubert v. Merrell Dow Pharmaceuticals. Connecticut Law Review* 30:1147–98.

Spon, R. D. 1998. Juvenile justice: A work "in progress." *Regent University Law Review* 10:29–51.

Stein, R. A. 1997. Probate reformation: The impact of the uniform laws. *Probate Lawyer* 23:1–21.

Stein, T. J. 1991. *Child welfare and the law.* New York: Longman.

Stith, K. 1993 The government interest in criminal law: Whose interest is it anyway? In S. E. Gottlieb, ed., *Public values in constitutional law,* pp. 137–70. Ann Arbor: University of Michigan Press.

Stolle, D. P. and D. B. Wexler. 1997. Therapeutic jurisprudence and preventive law: A combined concentration to invigorate the everyday practice of law. *Arizona Law Review* 39:25–33.

Strasburger, L. H., T. G. Gutheil, and A. Brodsky. 1997. On wearing two hats: Role conflict in serving as both psychotherapist and expert witness. *American Journal of Psychiatry* 154:448–56.

Stromberg, C. et al. 1988. *The psychologist's legal handbook.* Washington, D.C.: Council for National Register of Health Service Providers in Psychology.

Sunstein, C. R. 1996. *Legal reasoning and political conflict.* New York: Oxford University Press.

Swenson, L. C. 1993. *Psychology and law.* Pacific Grove, Calif.: Brooks/Cole.

Tesler, P. H. 1999. Collaborative law: What it is and why family law attorneys need to know about it. *American Journal of Family Law* 13:215–25.

Towle, Charlotte. 1961. Social work: Cause and function. *Social Casework* 42(8): 385–97.

Tribe, Lawrence. 1988. *American constitutional law.* 2d ed. Mineola, N.Y.: Foundation Press.

Tsai, B. 2000. The trend toward specialized domestic violence courts: Improvements on an effective innovation. *Fordham Law Review* 23:1285–1327.

Tyler, T. R. 1992. The psychological consequences of judicial procedures: Implications for civil commitment hearings. *Southern Methodist University Law Review* 46:433–45.

Ulman, J. N. 1933. Law as a creative force in social welfare. *Proceedings of the National Conference on Social Work, Detroit, Michigan, June 11–17.* Chicago: University of Chicago Press.

Vandevelde, K. J. 1998. *Thinking like a lawyer: An introduction to legal reasoning.* Boulder, Colo.: Westview.

Ventrell, M. R. 1995. The child's attorney: Understanding the role of zealous advocate. *Family Advocate* 17:73–76.

Wexler, D. B. 1990. *Therapeutic jurisprudence: The law as a therapeutic agent.* Durham, N.C.: Carolina Academic Press.

Wexler, D. B. and B. J. Winick, eds. 1996. *Law in a therapeutic key: Developments in therapeutic jurisprudence.* Durham, N.C.: Carolina Academic Press.

Winfield, R. D. 1995. *Law in a civil society.* Lawrence: University Press of Kansas.

Winick, B. J. 1991. Competency to consent to treatment: The distinction between assent and objection. *Houston Law Review* 28:15–62.

Wren, C. G. and J. R. Wren. 1986. *The legal research manual: A game plan for legal research and analysis.* 2d ed. Madison, Wisc.: Adams and Ambrose.

Yenney, S. L. and American Psychological Association Practice Directorate. 1994. *Business strategies for a caring profession.* Washington, D. C.: American Psychological Association.

Zirogiannis, L. 2001. Alienated children in divorce: Evidentiary issues with parental alienation syndrome. *Family Court Review* 39:334–41.

CASES AND LAWS CITED

Adoption and Safe Families Act, 42 U.S.C. 1305 (1997).

Bird v. W.C.W., 868 S.W.2d 767 (Sup. Ct. Tex. 1994).

Bowers v. Hardwick, 478 U.S. 186 (1986).

Bush v. Gore, 531 U.S. 98 (2000).

Civil Justice Reform Act, 28 U.S.C. 471–82 (1990).

Collignon v. Milwaukee County, 163 F.3d 982 (7th Cir. 1998).

Daubert v. Merrell Dow Pharmaceuticals, 509 U.S. 579 (1993).

DeShaney v. Winnebago County Department of Social Services, 489 U.S. 189 (1989).

Employee Retirement Income Security Act (ERISA), P.L. 93–406 (1974).

Erie Railroad v. Tompkins, 304 U.S. 64 (1938).

Estelle v. Gamble, 429 U.S. 97 (1976).

Falco v. Institute of Living, 254 Conn. 321 (2000).

Fraser v. United States, 236 Conn. 625 (1996).

Goldberg v. Kelly 397 U.S. 254 (1970).

Goss v. Lopez, 419 U.S. (1975).

In re Gault, 387 U.S. 1 (1967).

Jaffe v. Redmond, 518 U.S. 1 (1996).

Juvenile Court Act, Ill. Laws 131–37 (1899).

Kumho Tire v. Carmichael, 526 U.S. 137 (1999).

Legal Services Corporation v. Velazquez, 531 U.S. 533 (2001).

Lochner v. New York, 198 U.S. 45 (1905) (Holmes, J., dissenting).

Marbury v. Madison, 5 U.S. 137 (1803).

McCulloch v. Maryland, 17 U.S. 316 (1819).

Roland Machinery Co. v. Dresser Industries, Inc., 749 F.2d 380 (7th Cir. 1984).

Romer v. Evans, 517 U.S. 620 (1996).

Schrempf v. State, 487 N.E.2d 883 (N.Y. 1985).

State v. Hopper, 917 P.2d 872 (Kan. 1996).

State v. Saunders, 695 A.2d 722 (N.J. Super. Ct. App. Div. 1997).

State v. Wetherhorn, 683 P.2d 269 (Alaska Ct. App. 1984).

Steele v. Choi, 82 F.3d 175 (7th Cir. 1996).

Tarasoff v. Board of Regents, 17 Cal. 3d 425. (1976).

Texas Department of Community Affairs v. Burdine, 450 U.S. 248 (1981).

Troxel v. Granville, 530 U.S. 57 (2000).

United States v. Lopez, 514 U.S. 549 (1995).

United States v. Morrison, 529 U.S. 598 (2000).

Violent Crime Control and Law Enforcement Act of 1994 (often called the Three Strikes Law), 18 U.S.C. 3559c (2001).

Youngblood v. Romeo, 457 U.S. 307 (1982).

Zablocki v. Redhail, 434 U.S. 374 (1978).

INDEX

Abandonment. *See* Termination, clinical

Abortion, 20–21

Abuse. *See* Child welfare

Access to legal system, 77

Advanced directives, 120–121; mental health advance directives, 121

Addiction. *See* Drug courts; Specialized courts

Administration in social work, 137–138

Administrative law, 45; and exhaustion of remedies, 100; *see also* Law making

Adoption, 22–23

Adversarial system, 10, 63–64; and family law, 63, 112

Advocacy, 48, 107; in family court, 110

Affirmative action, 139

Agency liability. *See* Vicarious liability

AIDS. *See* HIV/AIDS

Alternative dispute resolution, 10, 33–35, 64; and divorce, 34; as mandatory process, 85

American Bar Association, Model Rules of Professional Conduct, 60–66

Americans with Disability Act, 140

Analogies in the law, 70

Apologies in legal cases, 10

Appellate review, 95; interlocutory appeal, 95

Aquinas, Saint Thomas, 18–19

Arbitration, 34

Attorney-client privilege. *See* Privileged communication

Attorneys, roles and expectations of, 58–59; *see also* Lawyers

Austin, John, 21

Balance of power, 41

Bentham, Jeremy, 20

Best interests of child standard, 112; *see also* Child welfare

Best practices, 72, 125

Behavioral decision theory (BDT), 23–24

Beyond a reasonable doubt, 50

Bill of Rights. *See* Constitutional law

Boundaries, 70

Breach of contract. *See* Contracts

Burden of production, 49, 87

Burden of proof, 49–50

Business issues for social workers, 143–150; *see also* Private practice

Cardozo, Benjamin, 54
Case law, 13–15, 152–154; citations, 15; elements of, 13–24; holding, 15; naming of cases, 14; parts of, 15; precedent, 14; publication of, 14; research strategies, 153; variation in, 5
Case records. *See* Records
Certiorari. *See* Writ of certiorari
Checks and balances, 39
Child abuse/neglect. *See* Child welfare
Child custody: and role of mental health professionals, 114–115; visitation, 7–8
Children: and legal representation, 110, 112–113; *see also* Lawyers for children
Child welfare, 115–118; Constitutional rights, 102; best interests standard, 109; criminal cases in, 116; elements of abuse case, 117; history of, 117–118; legal rules in, 73; permanency planning, 115; parents' rights, 115; reasonable efforts, 115, 117; reporting laws, 117; role of lawyers in, 116–117; termination of parental rights, 114–115, 117
Civil rights, 44–45, 47, 74, 98, 104; legal actions and, 104; professional discretion and, 74; Section 1983 lawsuits, 104
Civil Rights Act of 1964, 139
Civil suits, 48–50; burden of proof, 92; burden of production, 92; clear and convincing standard, 92; class-action lawsuits, 9; elements, 91; preponderance of evidence, 92
Clear and convincing evidence, 50, 92
Clinical social work practice: abandonment, 78–80; threatening clients and, 79

Code of ethics. See National Association of Social Workers
Collaborative law, 35, 64
Common law, 15, 45, 54–57
Competency, 61
Confidentiality: and child abuse cases, 116; and child custody, 114; professional duty, 126; Constitutional bases of, 126
Conflict of interest, 60
Constitutional amendments: First Amendment, 46–47, 99; Second Amendment, 97; Fourth Amendment, 105; Fifth Amendment, 99, 105; Sixth Amendment, 49, 105; Tenth Amendment, 41; Fourteenth Amendment, 99
Constitutional law, 40–45, 96–107; Bill of Rights, 41, 97, 99–100, 105; commerce clause, 44; development of, 97; due process, 41, 98; equality, 98; Equal Protection Clause, 102–104; fundamental rights, 101; individual rights, 41; interpretation of, 97–98; and juvenile courts, 106–107; liberty rights, 97–99; privacy rights, 101–102; procedural due process, 99–100; and social policy, 96; scrutiny, 101; state, 41; strict structure of, 96; substantive due process, 101–102; as the ultimate legal authority, 40–41, 97; Warren Court, 96
Contingency fees, 80
Contract law: acceptance of offer, 131–132; breach of contract, 133; changed circumstances, 134; and clients, 135; coercion, 134; consideration, 132; damages, 134;

duress, 134; fraud, 134; freedom to contract, 131, 134; intent, 132; liquidated damage clauses, 133; loss, 133; offer, 131–133; partial performance, 133; reasonable person standard, 132; reliance, 132–133; verbal agreements, 134

Courts: barriers to, 142; public and the, 143

Courtroom testimony. *See* Testimony

Criminal law, 48–50, 104–107; appointment of attorney in, 49; elements of, 48, 104, 108; government role in, 194; probable cause, 41, 105; standard of proof in, 93, 104

Critical legal studies, 31–33; and literary criticism, 31

Cultural bias in the law, 32

Custody. *See* Child custody; Family court

Damages, 94; in contract cases, 135; in tort cases, 128; punitive, 94

Delegation of power, 41

Depositions, 9–10, 83–84; *see also* Litigation process

Dicta, 15, 56

Directed verdict, 93

Disability law, 140–141

Discovery process, 80–84; *see also* Litigation process

Discretion: history of, 73–74; judges and, 57, 76; mental health and, 74; prisoners and, 74; social workers and, 72–76; welfare rights and, 74

Discrimination, 87, 103–104; employment, 139–140; in family courts, 111; and sexual orientation, 103

Dissenting opinions, 15

Divorce mediation, 34–35; *see also* Child custody,

Domestic partnerships. *See* Homosexuality

Domestic violence courts, 122–123; distinguished from traditional courts, 122; orientation of, 122

Double jeopardy, 105

Drug courts, 121–122; composition of, 122; eligibility for, 121; relapses and, 122

Due process, 41, 75; employment law and, 141; procedural due process, 99–100; substantive due process, 101–102; welfare rights and 74; *see also* Constitutional law

Duty to warn, 16, 55

Dworkin, Ronald, 29–31

Economics and the law, 27–29

Elder law, 61; legal rules and, 73; self-determination value in, 73

Elder care manager and liability, 7

Employer liability. *See* Vicarious liability

Employment law, 138–141; affirmative action, 139; benefits, 139; disability law, 140–141; discrimination laws, 87, 139–140; independent contractors, 139; reasonable accommodations, 141; termination of employees, 141

Enlightenment period, 19

Enumerated powers, 43

Equal Employment Opportunity Act, 139

Equality, 47

Equal protection. *See* Constitutional law

Equitable relief, 84, 94
ERISA (Employees' Retirement
    Income Security Act), 43
Ethic of care in law, 38
Ethics, 72; basis for advocacy, 96; and
    expert witnesses, 92–93; and
    managed care contracts, 136
Evidence, 87–89; authentification of,
    89; and burden of proof, 49–50;
    hearsay, 88; materiality, 87–88;
    prejudicial, 88; public policy
    exclusions, 88; and privilege, 88;
    relevance, 87–88
Ex parte motion, 84
Expert testimony, 90–93; and ethical
    concerns, 92–93; Daubert Standard,
    91–92; offer of proof, 91; purpose of,
    90; qualifications of an expert,
    91–92; social workers as, 92–93

Fact witness. See Testimony
Family court, 110–112; divorce and
    custody, 113–115; guardian ad litem,
    113; motion practice in, 113;
    parenting plans, 113; parent rights
    in, 114–115; social work advocacy
    role in, 114; see also Best interests of
    child standard; Child custody
Family law. See Adoption; Child
    welfare; Divorce
Federal court structure, 52–53; circuit
    courts, 52; district courts, 52;
    diversity jurisdiction, 52; subject
    jurisdiction, 52; Supreme Court
    jurisdiction, 52–53
Federal government: criminal law and,
    44; enumerated powers, 43
Federalism, 44–45
Feminist legal studies, 31
Fiduciary, 60–61
First principles. See Values

Formalism, 23–25
Fourteenth amendment. See
    Constitutional law
Fraud, 7
Freedom of speech, 47
Full Faith and Credit Cause. See
    Constitutional law

Guardianship, 38, 61
Gay/lesbian. See homosexuality
Gender discrimination, 47
Grand jury, 105
Group practice, 146–147; corporations
    and, 148–150; limited liability
    corporation (LLC), 149; operating
    agreements, 149; partnership
    agreements, 147; professional
    service corporation (PC), 148–149;
    see also Private practice
Group therapy: and
    confidentiality/privacy, 4–5, 40
Guardian ad litem, 113
Guardianship. See probate court

Hart, H. L. A., 21–22
Health insurance. See Managed care
Hearsay evidence: defined, 88
Hindsight bias, 87
HIV/AIDS, 69–70; and legal
    advocacy, 9
Holmes, Oliver Wendell, 25, 125, 127
Homosexuality, 103; and
    confidentiality, 126

Immunity: child abuse reporting, 117
Impairment of professional. See
    Vicarious liability
Incorrect treatment. See Malpractice
Independent contractor, 71
Inductive reasoning process, 15–16
Informed consent, 135

Insurance. *See* Managed care
Integrity of law, 30–31
Intentional torts, 124; defamation, 130; elements of, 129; fraud, 130; intentional infliction of emotional distress, 129; and punitive damages, 127
Interprofessional skills, 10–11
Interstate commerce clause. *See* Constitutional law
Involuntary civil commitment, 74
Issue spotting, 66, 69, 152

Jefferson, Thomas, 42
Joint custody. *See* Child custody
Judges: appellate level, 55; bench trials, 85; and decision-making process, 64, 93; deference to, 18; and legal rules, 56–57; and moral reasoning, 20–21; and philosophy, 17; as policy makers, 28; and problem-solving role, 26; role in specialized courts, 35
Judicial activisim, 30, 98
Judicial restraint, 26–27
Judicial review, 42–43
Juries, 85–86; in criminal cases, 105; deliberation of, 93–94; exclusion of potential jurors, 86; selection of, 86; *see also* Litigation process
Jurisdiction, 51–53, 81
Jury instructions, 93
Juvenile court system, 106–107; best practices in, 107; criminal offenses, 106; parens patriae doctrine, 106; progressive era reforms, 106; transfers to adult court, 107

Langdell, Christopher Columbus, 23
Law: and liability, 3; as a creative force, 11

Lawmaking, 40–48; and administrative agencies, 45; and courts, 51–54; and legislatures, 45
Lawyers, advocacy role, 58–59; communication with, 62; comparison to social workers, 59; competition and, 65; confidentiality, 62; contingency fees, 80; education of, 64–65; and image, 10, 58; loyalty to clients, 58, 60–61; personalities of, 63; power and authority of, 59; preparation of, 64–65; professionalism, 65; retainers, 80; right to counsel, 105; rules of conduct, 60–66; and selection of legal roles, 64; skills of practice, 66–68; socialization of, 18; social status of, 58; specialization of, 65; stereotyped image of, 58; thinking like a, 3; work product and, 61
Lawyers for children, 112–113; duty of child's lawyer, 113
Legal privilege. *See* Privileged communication
Legal reasoning, 3–4, 17–18, 68–71; analogical reasoning, 68, 70–71; deductive reasoning, 23–24, 30; and fact gathering, 69; inductive reasoning, 25–26; steps in, 68–69
Legal reform movements, 17, 18
Legal research, 65, 151; developing research questions, 152–153; electronic research, 154–156
Legal rules, 5–6, 16, 39–40, 45–46, 109; social work practice and, 72–73
Legal services: access to, 77; for the poor, 77, 111
Legislation: codification of, 20; legislative history, 23; legislative intent, 7; subordinate legislation, 45

Legislative supremacy doctrine, 45
Lesbian. *See* Homosexuality
Levi, Edward, 68
Liberty, 29–30, 98–99
Litigation process, 77–95; affirmative
 defense, 83; answer to the
 complaint, 83; closing statements,
 93; depositions, 83–84; directed
 verdict, 93; discovery, 80–84;
 jurisdiction, 81–82; jury
 selection, 85–86; mandatory
 dispute resolution and, 85;
 opening statements, 86; pleadings
 stage, 80–84; post-trial motions,
 94–95; preliminary injunction,
 84–85; pretrial, 81–84;
 production of evidence, 87;
 remedies, 94; settlement, 84;
 and themes, 86
Locke, John, 19

Magistrates, 51
Malpractice, 55; abandonment and,
 77–80; confidentiality and, 126;
 defined, 126; legal representation
 and, 80; private practice and, 144;
 risk reduction approach, 130; sexual
 impropriety and, 70; standard of
 care, 72, 124, 126; supervision and,
 69–70
Managed care, 84–85, 135–137; and
 abandonment, 137; and co-pay
 policies, 137; ERISA preemption,
 43; gag provisions, 136; and
 informed consent, 135; no cause
 terminations, 136; and treatment
 plans, 137
Mandated reporting of child abuse, 117;
 see also Child welfare
Marshall, John, 42

McCulloch v. Maryland, 41, 43
Mediation, 34–35; *see also* Alternative
 dispute resolution
Mental illness. *See* Involuntary civil
 commitment
Minors. *See* Children
Miranda warning, 49
Mistrial, 93
Motion to dismiss, 83, 93
Motion to quash, 82

Narratives, 67–68, 86–87, 93
National Association of Social Workers
 (NASW): Code of Ethics, 96;
 Committee on Inquiry, 7
Natural law, 18–20
Neglect of children. *See* Child welfare
Negligence, 49, 124; breach of duty,
 124, 127; causation, 127; comparative
 negligence, 128–129; contributory
 negligence, 128–129; damages, 128;
 defenses to, 128–129; duty of care,
 82, 125; forseeability of harm,
 125–126; injuries, 127–128; qualified
 immunity, 129; reasonable person
 standard, 126; respondeat superior
 doctrine, 127; scope of duty, 127;
 sovereign immunity, 129; statute of
 limitations,129; third-party liability,
 126; *see also* Best practices;
 Malpractice
Newton, Sir Isaac, 19

Oppression, 110

Paper Chase, 64
Parents: in child welfare cases,
 115–116; parens patriae doctrine,
 106; parental rights in family
 court, 114–115

Parental alienation syndrome,
91–92, 114
Philosophy of law, 17
Pleadings. *See* Litigation process
Policy advocacy, 11
Positivism, 21–22
Posner, Richard, 27–28
Postmodernism, 31–32
Pound, Roscoe, 25
Power of attorney, 120: durable power,
120; springing power, 120
Precedence, 15, 54–55; and court
hierarchy, 55; dictum, 56;
distinguishing, 56
Predictability in the law, 109, 112
Preemption, 43
Pretrial conference, 83
Preventive law, 10, 37–38, 64
Prisoner rights, 74,
Privacy rights, 101–102, 115; *see also*
Constitutional law
Private practice, 143–150;
corporations, 148–149; and debts,
144; establishing a practice,
143–144; group practice options,
146–150; limited liability,
144–145; loan guarantees,
144–145; partnerships, 147; pass-
through tax status, 145; sole
proprietorship, 146
Privileged communication, 4–5, 40;
attorney/client, 61–62; and evidence
law, 152; exception to, for legal
defense, 81; explanation of, 4–5;
and groups, 4–5
Probable cause, 41, 105
Probate Court, 118–121; abuses in, 19;
advance directives, 120–121;
capacity, 121; competency, 119;
conservatorship, 120; development
of, 118; durable power of attorney,
120; fiduciary, 119–120; guardianship, 119, 120; least intrusive
alternative, 119; power of
attorney, 120; role of social
worker in, 119; springing power
of attorney, 120
Procedural due process; *see*
Constitutional law
Professional organizations: and
standards of care, 72
Public defender, 8–9
Public policy rationale, 4
Punitive damages, 94

Race. *See* discrimination
Racial profiling, 74–75
Reasonable efforts requirement, 116;
see also Child welfare
Reasonable person standard, 126
Recovered memories, and
malpractice, 126
Records, case, 127
Reporting laws. *See* Child welfare
Respectable minority rule. *See*
Malpractice
Respondeat superior doctrine. *See*
Supervision; Vicarious liability
Restraining orders, 47
Rights theory, 29–31
Right to privacy. *See*
Constitutional law
Risk assessment. *See* Child welfare
Rule of law, 12

Search warrant, 105
Section 1983 liability. *See* Civil rights
Securities and Exchange
Commission, 44
Separation of powers, 39

Settlements of lawsuits: confidentiality in, 78; *see also* Litigation process

Social jurisprudence, 25

Social justice, 98

Social Sciences: and empirical evidence, 26; and legal outcomes, 26

Social Workers: advocacy role and constitutional law, 98, 107; and legal knowledge, 98; comparison to lawyers, 59; legal discretion, 74; professional judgment, 72–76; *see also* Discretion

Socratic method, 64–65

Sole proprietorship. *See* Private practice

Sovereign immunity, 56

Specialized courts, 110, 121–123

Stalking laws, 46–48

Standard of care, 72, 126–127; *see also* Malpractice

Standard of proof, 93–94

Stare decisis, 54–56; *see also* Precedence

State court structure, 51; appellate courts, 51; general jurisdiction courts, 51; limited jurisdiction courts, 51; supreme courts, 51

Statute of limitations, 81–82, 128

Statutory law: annotated statutes, 13, 152; classification system for, 11–13, 152; definition of terms, 12; interpretation of, 12–13; jurisdiction of, 42; policy considerations in, 13; public law number system, 11; reading statutes, 11–13; search strategies for locating, 152; statement of purpose, 12

Strict constructionists, 97–98; *see also* Constitutional law

Strict liability, 124

Subordinate legislation. *See* Legislation

Substantive due process. *See* Constitutional law

Suicide, 85–87; *see also* Duty to protect

Summons, 82

Supervision: and contract law, 132; and liability, 69–70

Supreme Court, 52–53, scope of authority, 52; *see also* Constitutional law

Systems theory, 109

Tarasoff case, 15, 16, 55

Termination: clinical, 81; abandonment, 78–80

Termination of parental rights. *See* Child welfare

Testimony, 89–93; cross examination, 90; Daubert standard, 91–92; direct examination, 89–90; of fact witness, 88–90; foundation questions, 89; leading questions, 89; social workers as, 91–92; subpoena process, 89; *see also* Expert testimony

Therapeutic Jurisprudence (TJ), 10, 36–37, 64; and interdisciplinary approaches, 36

Thinking like a lawyer, 5

Third-party payers. *See* Managed care

Three strikes law, 94

Tort law, 124; categories of, 124; defined, 124; as distinguished from criminal law, 124; and legal lottery, 125; purposes of, 124–125; and social control, 130; as supporting safe practice, 130; *see also* Intentional torts; Negligence; Strict liability

Towle, Charlotte, 2

Trier of fact: defined, 85

Twinkie defense, 91

Ulman, Joseph, 11

United States Constitution. *See*
Constitutional law

Values: and constitutional law, 96–104;
equality, 29, 102–104; first
principles, 18, 30–31, 60–66, 105;
freedom, 29–30; of lawyers, 60–66
Vicarious liability, 127; *see also*
Supervision
Voir dire, 85–86

Welfare rights, 74
Wexler, David, 36
Whistle-blower, 153
Witness. *See* Expert testimony;
Litigation process;
Testimony
Women and equality, 46–47
Writ of certiorari, 52

Zealous representation, 62–63